PCI Hot-Plug Application and Design

The Comprehensive Guide to Designing PCI Hot-Plug Systems

Includes and Exceeds Information from
PCI Hot-Pug Specification, Revision 1.0

Written by
Alan Goodrum
Compaq Fellow
Compaq Computer Corporation

Reviewed by
Edward Solari

Annabooks

San Diego

PCI Hot-Plug Application and Design

Alan Goodrum

Published by
Annabooks
11838 Bernardo Plaza Court
San Diego, CA 92128-2414
USA

619-673-0870

Printed in the United States of America

ISBN 0-929392-60-4

First Printing March 1998

Information provided in this publication is derived from various sources, standards, and analyses. Any errors or omissions shall not imply any liability for direct or indirect consequences arising from the use of this information. The publisher, authors, and reviewers make no warranty for the correctness or for the use of this information, and assume no liability for direct or indirect damages of any kind arising from technical interpretation or technical explanations in this book, for typographical or printing errors, or for any subsequent changes.

The publisher and authors reserve the right to make changes in this publication without notice and without incurring any liability.

All trademarks mentioned in this book are the property of their respective owners. Annabooks has attempted to properly capitalize and punctuate trademarks, but cannot guarantee that it has done so properly in every case.

Dedication

This book is dedicated to the two groups of people who supported me before and during its writing. It is dedicated first to the dozens of people at Compaq who helped develop PCI hot-plug technology and bring it to market. Secondly, it is dedicated to my wife, Debbie, and children, Ryan, Kyle, and Laura, who don't always understand what Dad does all day, but know all too well how much time it sometimes takes. My thanks to both groups who allowed me the time to write this book.

Alan Goodrum

Houston, Texas

Contents

Figures

Tables

Preface

Over the past decade a new class of business machinery has emerged— the standards-based server. Leveraging the economies of scale of the personal computer industry, this class of machine has advanced far beyond its original "personal" roots. Today's servers often use multiple microprocessors, each with performance several orders of magnitude greater than their ancestors of a decade ago. Storage systems once measured in the tens of megabytes can now be measured in terabytes.

With the growth of robust operating systems such as Novell IntranetWare, Microsoft Windows NT, and x86 versions of Unix from Santa Cruz Operation (SCO), the standards-based server has become an essential piece of business infrastructure. Anxious to take advantage of the dramatic reduction in the price/performance ratio of such systems, businesses have enthusiastically transferred to standards-based servers data and applications essential to their day-to-day operation.

Essential business applications require much more than faster hardware, more storage, and different operating systems. As businesses depend more upon their servers, reliability and manageability have become more important. Company-wide local-area networks and email systems, first implemented for convenience, have become mission-critical applications. Loss of the network for even short periods of time can have enormous impact on a company's operation. Furthermore, the need to simplify system management and the availability of higher performance servers have enabled consolidation of multiple smaller servers into fewer more powerful ones. This trend multiplies the need for constant availability as each downtime event affects more and more people in bigger and bigger ways.

Server hardware and software manufacturers have responded to the demand for more reliable systems by introducing hardware redundancy and expanded system management tools. Redundant arrays of independent disks (RAID) storage systems protect critical data in the least reliable subsystem, the mechanical operation of the disk drives. RAID systems commonly include hot-plug drives that enable the user to replace the failed component or expand storage capacity without interrupting the overall operation of the server. Error-correcting memory subsystems protect system operation against random memory errors. Redundant power supplies, backup processor cards, redundant network interface cards (NICs), and even schemes for one system to fail and transfer all operation to a different system have all been introduced to reduce the occurrence or length of downtime events.

The next step on the road to increased availability of servers is in the I/O subsystem. Since its introduction in 1992, the PCI local bus has become the most widely used I/O bus in standards-based server systems. Compaq Computer Corporation recognized the need for defining a standard way to remove and install standard PCI adapter cards without powering-off the server. In June 1996 Compaq approached the Steering Committee of the PCI Special Interest Group (PCI SIG) to form a workgroup to develop such a standard. The workgroup was immediately formed with Compaq as the chair. The amazing unity among the workgroup member companies, and the speed at which the first draft of the specification was published, testify to the recognition in the industry of the need for PCI hot-plug capabilities. Draft 0.9 of the *PCI Hot-Plug Specification* was made public in March of 1997, nine months after the Steering Committee chartered the workgroup. Formal release of the specification by the PCI Steering Committee occurred in October of 1997.

This book is first of all a complete presentation of the content of the *PCI Hot-Plug Specification*. Each of the requirements of the specification is presented. Where appropriate, additional background information is presented that explains why the specification was written as it was, or possible consequences of non-compliance. This book is not intended to replace the specification. The ultimate authority on PCI hot-plug operations remains the official specification. However, reading this book prior to or concurrently with the specification should improve your understanding of the requirements of the specification. You are assumed to be familiar with the *PCI Local Bus Specification, Revision 2.1*.

In addition to presenting the content of the specification, this book also includes application information that is beyond the scope of the specification. Chapter 7 discusses the hardware implemented in Compaq's first product designed to this specification, the ProLiant 6500, as an example of platform hardware. Chapter 8 discusses how the specification is addressed in the first products from Novell, Microsoft, and SCO.

The author gratefully acknowledges the massive team effort on the part of numerous Compaq employees who designed, implemented, and tested the first products built according to the *PCI Hot-Plug Specification*. Additionally, several people made specific contributions to this book. Bob Periera provided the safety agency requirements. Dragos Tapu created the drawings of the mechanical implementation of PCI hot-plug technology in the ProLiant 6500. Dan Zink and Jeff Autor provided the information and reviewed the IntranetWare section of Chapter 7. Jeff Galloway did the same for the Windows NT 4.0 section, and Tom Rhodes for the SCO UnixWare 7 section. Lastly, Barry Basile contributed portions of the ProLiant 6500 Hot-Plug Controller description, and both he and Rich Waldorf spent many hours reviewing the majority of the manuscript.

The author would also like to thank Ed Solari who helped establish the early direction and focus of the book, and helped craft the final product to meet that direction and focus.

Alan Goodrum
Compaq Fellow,
Compaq Computer Corporation

and

Chairman, PCI Hot-Plug Workgroup

Terminology

In most places in this book the *PCI Hot-Plug Specification, Revision 1.0* is referred to as the Hot-Plug Spec. In most places the *PCI Local Bus Specification, Revision 2.1* is referred to as "PCI 2.1."

The following terminology in this book has been kept consistent with the Hot-Plug Spec:

Hot-plugging in all its various verb forms refers to the process of inserting or removing a piece of hardware from a system without stopping the software or powering-down the system as a whole. The process may include stopping a portion of the software or powering-down a portion of the hardware. A hot-plug operation can be either a *hot-insertion* or a *hot-removal.*

A *PCI adapter card* (or simply *adapter card* when the context makes it unambiguous) is an expansion board designed according to the PCI Local Bus Specification to be plugged into a PCI slot. A PCI adapter card generally includes at least one PCI device, but is not required to (*e.g.,* a multiple-card set may include a PCI device on only one of the cards).

An *adapter driver* is the software device driver for an adapter card.

A *slot* refers to a location into which an adapter card can be plugged. A slot designed to allow hot-plugging of the adapter card is called a *hot-plug slot.* Slots not designed for hot-plug operations are called *conventional slots.*

The terms *PCI device* or simply *device* without additional adjectives refer to a hardware component that contains a PCI Configuration Space header, and that can be connected electrically to a PCI bus. A device can be installed permanently as part of the platform hardware, or it can be a part of an adapter card.

The terms *transaction* or *bus transaction* refer to the operations performed on the PCI bus that generally transfer data between masters and targets. Some transactions terminate without transferring data.

The *platform* refers to the system hardware. It includes the chassis, CPU, memory, and common I/O devices such as keyboards and monitors. Platforms of interest to this book also include a bridge from the CPU bus to the PCI bus, and slots into which PCI adapter cards can be plugged. A *hot-plug platform* includes at least one hot-plug slot. A *conventional platform* does not.

The terms *system* or *hot-plug system* used without additional adjectives refer to the combination of the hardware that includes the PCI slot and adapter card, and all the software for the application that uses it. In this context the system includes the platform, the adapter cards, the operating system with its device drivers, and application software.

PCI-based platforms are divided into a hierarchy of PCI bus segments. Each *bus segment* is connected to the other bus segments by *PCI-to-PCI bridges* (or bridges to other intervening buses). The bridges logically join the different bus segments so that transactions can pass from one bus segment to another, but keep them electrically isolated so that electrical characteristics of one bus segment do not effect other bus segments.

A hot-plug slot can be in one of two *states*, either *off* or *on*. Changing the *slot state* from off to on or vice versa is called turning off a slot or turning on a slot. Turning a slot off or on is a multiple-step operation that is defined in detail in the Hot-Plug Spec, and affects not only the power supplied to the slot, but also the states of the bus isolation devices and the RST# pin for the slot.

Before an adapter card can be hot-removed, the system must *quiesce* adapter activity. This operation is defined in detail in the Hot-Plug Spec, and involves stopping all software and hardware activity for the adapter.

As in the Hot-Plug Spec and PCI 2.1 a shorthand notation is used when referring to the operating frequency of the PCI bus. Operation up to 33 1/3 MHz is referred to simply as 33 MHz operation. Operation above 33 1/3 MHz up to 66 2/3 MHz is referred to as 66 MHz operation.

1. Introduction To PCI Hot-Plug Technology

Over the past decade, file and application servers based on the industry-standard personal computer architecture have undergone steady improvement in the areas of reliability and availability. Redundancy was first introduced in the least reliable subsystems, disk drives, main memory, and power supplies. Eventually some subsystems were further enhanced to be inserted and removed while the rest of the system remained operational, a process commonly referred to as hot-plugging.

While standards-based servers were making steady progress toward higher reliability and availability, the PCI bus burst onto the scene. Since the introduction of the *PCI Local Bus Specification, Revision 1.0* in 1992, the PCI bus has rapidly pervaded the computer industry. In the first five years after the publication of the specification the installed base of PCI adapter cards exploded to well over 100 million cards.

Once the least reliable subsystems (the disk drives and power supplies) had been improved with hot-plug capabilities, the next step for improving system availability was adding hot-plug capabilities to the I/O subsystem. The PCI bus was the natural place to start. The *PCI Hot-Plug Specification*[1] extended the capabilities of the *PCI Local Bus Specification, Revision 2.1*[2] (PCI 2.1), to enable standard PCI adapter cards to be inserted and removed in systems without turning off the system power.

Hot-plugging of I/O cards is not a new concept. For example, certain industrial markets such as the telephone equipment industry have used hot-plug subsystems for years. The Hot-Plug Spec brings hot-plug technology to the PCI bus, the bus that will likely be the mainstay for I/O cards for servers for years to come.

---

[1] *PCI Hot-Plug Specification, Revision 1.0*, October 6, 1997, PCI Special Interest Group, Portland, Oregon.
[2] *PCI Local Bus Specification, Revision 2.1*, June 1, 1995, PCI Special Interest Group, Portland, Oregon.

The PCI bus was originally designed to serve the personal and business computer markets. The size of this market has caused PCI components to achieve volumes that have also captured the attention of equipment manufacturers in smaller markets such as telecommunications and industrial computing. It is expected that the concepts employed to enable hot-plugging PCI adapter cards in standards-based servers are similarly applicable to other systems based on the PCI local bus.

1.1 Using Standard PCI Adapter Cards

The primary objective of PCI hot-plug technology is to increase the availability of server-class products that use standard PCI adapter cards. Constraining the solution to use standard PCI adapter cards has certain advantages and disadvantages. The primary advantages are that the solution works with the installed base of adapter cards, and doesn't splinter the future adapter card market into "hot-plug-capable" cards and "non-hot-plug-capable" cards. This leads to more rapid market acceptance of systems employing the technology.

The disadvantage of constraining the solution to use existing standard PCI adapter cards is that it limits the alternative implementations. The PCI 2.1 specification and its predecessors were not written to accommodate hot-plug operations. Many of the alternatives used to implement hot-plug cards on other I/O buses are unworkable with standard PCI adapter cards. For example, some hot-plug systems use variable-length connector pins to guarantee a sequence of connections as a card is inserted or removed. However, the PCI connector's card-edge "gold fingers" are specified to be all the same lengths. Although the mating connector could have been modified, the infinite variations in the size and shape of PCI adapter cards makes card-guide schemes difficult and expensive. Without a guide scheme there is a high probability that an adapter card could be inserted into the connector at an angle and short connections on the bus.

Furthermore, there is no provision in PCI 2.1 for isolating the bus signals on a device if its power is removed. Most digital logic I/O-buffer designs commonly used today include diode clamps both to ground and to the power pins. These diodes are designed to protect the device from electrostatic discharges (ESD) that could destroy the device. However, if a device with such input buffers is not powered (*i.e.*, the power pins are at 0 V), then the I/O pins will be clamped by the ESD diodes to near 0 V. Such a device could not be connected to a live PCI bus without interfering with PCI bus signaling.

Without the freedom of modifying the adapter card to optimize cost, a solution that impacts only the system-board design will inevitably have the disadvantage of higher cost. The Hot-Plug Spec requires all power and bus signals for each slot to be isolated for insertion and removal. The specification does not define how a platform will isolate these signals, but considering that there are over 45 bussed signals in the 32-bit version of the PCI connector, the cost of any solution will be a significant concern.

1.2 Who Needs PCI Hot-Plug Technology?

PCI hot-plug technology is not for everybody. The added cost of isolating each hot-plug slot from the bus must be weighed against the cost of system downtime.

The classes of applications that would typically derive a suitable benefit from PCI hot-plug technology are mission-critical applications with a high cost of downtime, applications that require continuous availability, or applications where a large number of users depend upon a single server. In many cases such applications could recover the increased system cost by avoiding only one or two unexpected downtime events.

On the other hand, single-user systems or systems that can be easily stopped at night or on weekends for maintenance would be less likely to benefit significantly from PCI hot-plug capabilities.

The following questions can be used as a guide in determining whether your application requires hot-plug capability:

1. Would a large number of users be affected if this application were not available?

2. Would there likely be significant other costs (*e.g.*, lost sales, lost productivity, etc.) if the application were not available?

3. Is it difficult to schedule a time for maintenance when no one is using the application?

In general, the more "yes" answers to the above questions, the more likely your application can justify the higher cost of PCI hot-plug capabilities.

1.3 What's Different from PCI 2.1 and What's Common?

1.3.1 Differences

A PCI hot-plug system differs from a conventional system in several areas.

- Isolation devices. The platform includes additional hardware for each hot-plug slot that enables all bus and power pins on that connector to be isolated from the rest of the system.
- Other hot-plug electrical hardware. The platform includes other electrical hardware for control and indication of hot-plug operations. This hardware is described in detail in Chapter 2.
- Hot-plug-ready operating system. The operating system must comprehend a device being removed or inserted while the system is running. Once the operating system allows this, special applications can be added to control turning slots on and off.
- Hot-plug-ready adapter drivers. In most cases hot-plug-ready operating systems will require changes in the device-driver model to allow them to be stopped and started while the system is running. Adapter card device drivers must be modified to conform to the new device-driver specification from the operating system vendor.
- System electrical and timing requirements. Most alternatives for bus isolation devices will affect the electrical and timing characteristics of the bus. The platform vendor must compensate for any negative effects on signal flight times. For example, the number of slots or the total length of the bus may have to be reduced.
- System mechanical design. Although the Hot-Plug Spec includes no requirements in this area, good design practice requires certain changes to the mechanical design of the

system to make PCI hot-plug capability useful. For example, the chassis will probably require new openings that provide access to the hot-plug slots, while restricting access to hazardous areas. Other changes would also be required to simplify the user's access to one card, while protecting adjacent cards from accidental shorting. See Chapter 6 for other examples.

1.3.2 Commonality

Hot-plug systems must have many things in common with conventional systems, if they are to use the same adapter cards.

- Same bus protocol. PCI signaling protocol is in no way affected by the presence of hot-plug slots. An adapter card should plug in and power-on in a hot-plug slot exactly the same way it plugs in and powers-on in a conventional slot.
- Signaling levels. Either 3.3 V or 5.0 V signaling can be used with hot-plug slots. The same slot keying mechanisms that are defined in PCI 2.1 apply as well.
- Power supply specifications. The same power supply voltage and tolerance specifications apply to hot-plug systems as well as conventional systems.
- Adapter card mechanical specifications. PCI hot-plug platforms accept standard PCI adapter card mechanical designs.
- Connector. The PCI 2.1 32- and 64-bit PCI connectors and their pinouts are used in PCI hot-plug platforms.
- Configuration Space. No changes are required in the Configuration Space.
- Slot electrical and timing requirements. The platform vendor must compensate for any changes in flight time caused by bus isolation devices. Therefore, the adapter card timing requirements remain the same in both hot-plug and conventional platforms.

1.4 What the *PCI Hot-Plug Specification* Controls

The Hot-Plug Spec does *not* specify every aspect of a hot-plug system. Instead the specification completely defines a few key areas, and then allows the suppliers of the various hardware and software components of the system to optimize the remaining areas of their design to fit the needs of their customers.

The Hot-Plug Spec focuses primarily on two interfaces, one hardware and one software, as shown in Figure 1-1. The figure illustrates a hot-plug system comprised of both conventional components and components unique to hot-plug systems. The Conventional System Software consists of the operating system, adapter drivers, and applications that are present in any system. In a system that fully supports PCI hot-plug technology, the operating system and drivers would be enhanced as described in Chapter 5 to allow devices to be removed and inserted while the system is running. The Conventional Platform Hardware consists of the CPU(s), the bridge to the PCI bus, and all of the standard components in a standards-based server, such as standard disk controllers, standard peripherals, and a bridge to an expansion bus. The PCI bus includes at least one hot-plug slot that accepts standard PCI adapter cards.

The cloud in the center of the figure represents the collection of hardware and software that are unique to a hot-plug system. It includes the control logic for powering-on and powering-off a slot, and a device driver for managing the control logic. The interfaces between the cloud and the rest of the system are the two interfaces standardized by the specification.

The first interface defined by the Hot-Plug Spec is the connection to the slot. In most respects this interface is a standard PCI slot. However, PCI 2.1 tacitly assumes that the whole system powers-on and powers-off together. Additional requirements of powering-on and powering-off a single slot while the rest of the system is running are beyond the scope of PCI 2.1. These requirements are covered in the Hot-Plug Spec, and are presented in Chapters 2, 3 and 4 of this book.

The second standard interface defined for PCI hot-plug is purely a software interface. It is the interface between the high-level hot-plug routines that include the user interface, and the low-level device driver that directly controls the hardware for powering-on and powering-off slots. This software interface will be presented in Chapter 5, and is referred to as the Hot-Plug Primitives.

1.4.1 Adapter Card Hardware

The Hot-Plug Spec provides a comprehensive list of adapter cards requirements beyond those of PCI 2.1. This isn't hard to do, since one of the fundamental objectives of the specification was to use standard adapter cards. Therefore the list of new requirements is short and complete. (See Chapter 4.) The combination of the *PCI Local Bus Specification* and the *PCI Hot-Plug Specification* completely specify how to build an adapter card for a PCI hot-plug system.

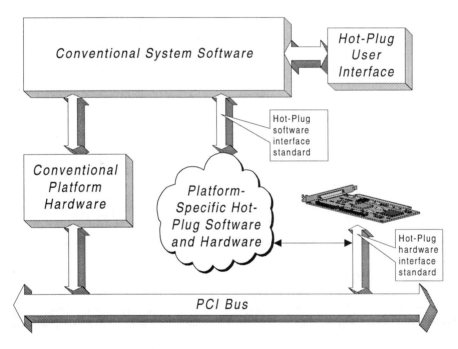

Figure 1-1 Standardized Hot-Plug Hardware and Software Interfaces

1.4.2 Platform Requirements

The Hot-Plug Spec describes the minimum hardware that the platform is required to include to guarantee that standard PCI adapter cards can be inserted and removed, and to support hot-plug software routines. These requirements are described in detail in Chapter 3. An abbreviated list follows:

- Slot-specific bus and power isolation devices.
- Control logic for powering-on and powering-off the slots.
- Software access to slot-specific information such as PRSNT[1:2]#, and M66EN.
- Slot-specific "attention indicators."

The specification does not require a particular implementation of any of these features; only that there be some implementation.

Many other aspects of the platform design are not standardized by the specification. The following aspects of the platform are left for the platform vendor to implement according to his customer's needs. Refer to Chapter 7 for an example of how these features are implemented in one product.

- The number of hot-plug slots, their physical locations within the chassis, and their logical locations within the PCI bus hierarchy.
- The characteristics of the bus isolation devices.
- The programming model for the control logic for powering-on and powering-off slots.
- Mechanisms for protecting a card from accidental removal from, or insertion into an active slot.
- Mechanical insertion and removal aids.

1.4.3 Operating System Requirements

It should come as no surprise to anyone that there are dramatic differences between the structures of different operating systems that are used in the industry served by the PCI local bus. While such diversity gives the customer a great deal of choice in his purchasing selection, it complicates the process of developing a standard that works equally well with any operating system. Furthermore, not only is it difficult to write a low-level software standard that applies equally well to different operating systems, there is little benefit to the customer in requiring each operating system to implement PCI hot-plug software routines in the same way.

In most cases the Hot-Plug Spec avoids this problem by specifying the *requirements* of the solution, rather than by specifying the solution itself. Some areas are left completely up to the operating system vendor to control. Other areas that require specification are assigned to the operating system vendor to specify. For example, the operating system vendor is responsible for determining what should happen to the file system if a critical disk controller is removed. Even higher-level hot-plug features are left up to the operating system vendor. The specification defines what is necessary for "hot-removal" and "hot-insertion." But the operating system vendor decides whether "hot-insertion" of completely new device is permitted (sometimes called "hot-addition"), or whether the system is limited to hot-inserting only cards that were previously hot-removed (sometimes called "hot-replacement"). Each operating system vendor is free to implement solutions that meet the demands of his market.

Although some software features affect only the operating system and can be left unspecified, other features affect software components supplied by other vendors, and therefore require a specification. But here again these features vary from one operating system to another, so a single industry standard would not be the right solution. The Hot-Plug Spec addresses these areas by requiring the operating system vendor to specify them. The following is an abbreviated list of the items that are specified by the operating system vendor. Refer to Chapter 5 for a detailed presentation of this topic. Examples of how the technology is implemented in several operating systems are presented in Chapter 8.

- Adapter driver specifications for quiescing adapter activity.
- The driver-level interface to the system hardware that controls powering-on and powering-off slots. This is the Hot-Plug Primitive interface presented in more detail in Chapter 5, section 5.7.
- How PCI resource configuration is handled.

1.5 Limitations of PCI Hot-Plug

PCI hot-plug technology has some notable limitations. These limitations generally result from the constraint of working with hardware and software that were designed before there was a need for hot-plugging PCI adapter cards. Neither the PCI bus, nor the operating systems commonly used in this class of systems were originally designed to tolerate hardware that suddenly failed or was removed while the system was running.

Limitation 1. A PCI hot-plug system is not intended to survive a component failure that violates the integrity of the PCI bus.

In systems employing the PCI bus today the PCI bus is a critical component. If a connection to the PCI bus were to become unreliable, there is no mechanism for the system to recover. Here are just a few examples of unrecoverable failures:

- If a device's connection were to break at a control signal such as FRAME#, the device might not respond when addressed by the CPU, and critical data could be lost.

- If an AD connection were to become unreliable, a bus master could produce erroneous addresses on a memory write transaction, and corrupt data or programs anywhere in main memory or other PCI devices.

- If a control signal such as IRDY# or TRDY# were to short to Vcc, the PCI bus protocol would hang in a transaction that could never complete. All subsequent use of that PCI bus segment would be blocked.

Since the system depends on the reliable operation of the PCI bus, the system will likely crash in these examples of bus failure, and in many others.

Although PCI hot-plug technology can improve the reliability of the system by allowing failed components to be replaced; it still depends upon the integrity of the PCI bus itself. To illustrate which kinds of failures can be tolerated and which kinds cannot, consider an example of a network interface controller (NIC). NIC hardware is commonly comprised of various layers of hardware. One such layer would include the drivers and receivers that connect electrically to the wires of the network. The next layer would include data queues and control logic for the network protocol. Another layer would contain the state machines and connections to the PCI bus. If a failure occurs in either of the first two layers, the failure might have no effect at all on the PCI bus. The rest of the system could be designed to detect such failures and continue running. However, if a failure occurs in the PCI interface, it could violate the integrity of the PCI bus, leading inevitably to a system crash.

Limitation 2. The user cannot remove an adapter card from the system until the software acknowledges that it is ready for him to do so.

In general, the software systems used in servers depend upon the integrity of the I/O device hardware. Although systems can be designed with redundant I/O subsystems that tolerate some kinds of failures, generally software at all levels— from the application, to the kernel, to the device driver— will not tolerate the sudden loss of an I/O device. Here are some examples of various levels of software and how they depend upon the I/O device.

- It is not uncommon for a device driver to test a hardware status bit in the device it controls by entering a short software loop waiting for a necessary value to appear. If a device suddenly fails (or is hot-removed), the necessary value might never appear, causing the device driver to hang in the wait loop forever.

- When the operating system's virtual memory manager detects a page fault, the memory manager is required to locate the requested page in a secondary storage device and load it into main memory. If the controller for the secondary storage device fails (or is hot-removed), then the operating system will not be able to schedule the routine to continue executing.

- When an application needs to get data from, or send data to a device, the operating system will typically suspend the application until the I/O operation completes. If the device fails (or is hot-removed) and hangs the device driver (as described above), the application might remain suspended forever.

PCI hot-plug protocol avoids problems with partially completed operations by requiring the user to warn the software before any hot-removal operation. This allows the software to gracefully shut down operations on the device before the device disappears. The process is presented in more detail in Chapter 5, and is called *quiescing adapter activity*. The Hot-Plug Spec does not state how or even if this rule is enforced. The most elaborate systems might implement protection mechanisms such as interlocks and trap doors that prevent the user from accessing adapter cards until they have been quiesced. More cost-sensitive systems might offer less protection. The most cost-sensitive systems might not enforce the rule at all, and trust the user to wait until the appropriate message appears on the console before removing the card.

> **Limitation 3. Cards can only be inserted into slots that have previously been turned off by some operation established by the system designer.**

In general, PCI adapter cards are designed to be inserted into a connector that is not powered. In other words, no provision is made to guard against problems such as arcing between contacts as connections are being made, or to guarantee that voltages are applied to power pins before signal pins to prevent device damage. PCI hot-plug protocol requires the system to turn off the slot before an adapter card can be inserted. While the Hot-Plug Spec defines in great detail the steps involved in turning off a slot, it does not define how the system will guarantee the slot is off before the user inserts a card. The most elaborate systems will implement protection mechanisms that automatically turn off a slot before a card can be inserted. However, more cost-sensitive systems might not enforce the rule at all, and trust the user to notify the software to turn off the slot before he inserts the card.

1.6 Relationship Between PCI Hot-Plug and PCI Power Management Technologies

The problems addressed by the *PCI Hot-Plug Specification* have some striking similarities, and some significant differences with another specification from the PCI Special Interest Group, the *PCI Power Management* specification. The most obvious similarity is that they both provide ways to turn the power off and on to some PCI devices while the rest of the system remains operational. This leads to significant similarity in the software that reinitializes and resumes using the devices.

But at this point the similarities end. The two specifications solve different problems that are present in different markets, and consequently require different implementations. The *PCI Power Management* specification enables the reduction of system power consumption, which is of most concern in the portable market and to a lesser extent the desktop market. System cost is of great concern in this market, and a solution that requires changes to the PCI devices is acceptable, if it produces a lower overall system cost.

Consequently the *PCI Power Management* specification defines a new set of registers inside the PCI device's Configuration Space for controlling power management functions. Power management software writes to these registers to change a device's power management state. One such state, $D3_{hot}$, is equivalent to applying RST# to the device and removing power, except that the device remains powered just enough to allow software to write to the device's Configuration Space again and power-on the device. A highly cost-effective solution is achieved by integrating the power management hardware inside the PCI device.

On the other hand, the *PCI Hot-Plug Specification* enables the insertion and removal of existing PCI adapter cards, while the system is running. No new registers can be added to PCI devices. Furthermore, the hardware for controlling the power state of the device must be located on the system side of the PCI connector, so the slot can be completely powered-off before the card is removed. Finally, the server market can afford to pay more for this solution, since improved system reliability and availability produces significant cost savings to the user.

Consequently the Hot-Plug Spec places a significant hardware burden on the platform to control power to the slots in such a way that standard PCI adapter cards can be removed and inserted while the rest of the system is running.

1.7 Relationship Between PCI Hot-Plug and ACPI

Another emerging industry standard, the Advanced Configuration and Power Interface (ACPI) specification, standardizes various aspects of managing power in a system. It defines standard system status and control registers for devices to signal their need for software assistance in controlling their power, and it defines a generic interpretive-code language for performing those control functions. Any subset of a system can be designed to have a reduced-power state, and can have control methods defined to enable the operating system to determine when the device is not being used, and to reduce its power consumption. Examples of subsets of the system that might have reduced-power states are:

- A single PCI device on the system board that includes registers that comply with the *PCI Power Management* specification, *e.g.*, the standard system SCSI controller.

- A single PCI device on a plug-in adapter card that includes registers that comply with the *PCI Power Management* specification, *e.g.*, a network interface controller plugged into a slot.

- A portion of the system board that has been partitioned into a separate power domain by the system-board designer, and given a unique power control port that software can control. For example, the keyboard and mouse controller might be grouped with the standard serial and parallel ports on one power plane. A power switch for this power plane could be controlled by a single I/O bit on a different power plane.

- A single PCI slot that has been partitioned into a separate power domain by the system-board designer, and given a unique power control port that software can control, *e.g.*, a PCI hot-plug slot.

Notice that the last example is precisely the capability that is defined by the Hot-Plug Spec. It is a means for the software to control the power of a subset of the system. Connecting the PCI hot-plug control logic to the ACPI status and control registers as prescribed by ACPI, and providing the appropriate interpretive-code control routines, enables a system that complies both with the ACPI specification and the Hot-Plug Spec to use PCI hot-plug hardware, not only for hot-removal and insertion, but for power management of a standard PCI adapter card as well.

2. PCI Hot-Plug Fundamentals

2.1 Hot-Plug System Components

Figure 2-1 illustrates the components of a hot-plug system and how they are related. A detailed discussion of each component follows.

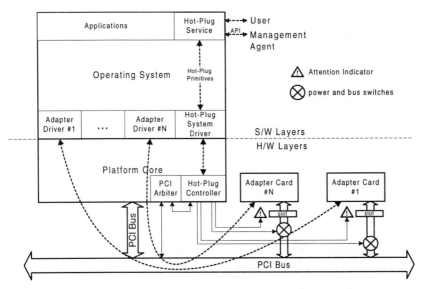

Figure 2-1: PCI Hot-Plug System Components

Adapter Card   A card designed according to the *PCI Local Bus Specification* to be installed in a PCI connector. PCI hot-plug technology accommodates almost any adapter card designed to the PCI 2.0 or 2.1 specifications. The only kinds of cards that might have problems are cards with unusual requirements, such as enormous decoupling capacitance (*e.g.*, >3000 µf on 5 V or 3.3 V), or multiple-card sets that must be powered-on and powered-off simultaneously. See Chapter 4 for a detailed presentation of adapter card requirements.

Adapter Driver   A software device driver to control the adapter card. The operating system vendor specifies the structure of the adapter driver both for hot-plug and conventional systems. A hot-plug-ready operating system will normally require changes to adapter drivers to make them hot-plug-ready. An adapter driver without such modifications would still load and operate as it always did, even with a hot-plug-ready operating system, but would not enable the adapter card to be hot-plugged.

Application   The main software function that the server is performing, *e.g.*, file serving or data base manipulation.

Attention Indicator   Each PCI hot-plug slot requires an indicator associated with it that, when activated, calls attention to the slot. Few details about the implementation of this indicator are defined in the Hot-Plug Spec, but the simplest implementation would be an LED located near the slot.

The Hot-Plug Spec does not define under what conditions the attention indicator must be illuminated, but rather it assigns that responsibility to the Hot-Plug Service.

Hot-Plug Controller

Logic that is responsible for controlling all of the hot-plug circuitry, including

- slot-specific bus and power isolation devices.
- slot-specific sensors for card presence (PRSNT[1:2]# pins) and frequency capability (M66EN pin).
- slot-specific indicators (required attention indicator and optional slot state indicator).

The detailed behavior of the Hot-Plug Controller and its programming model is not defined in the Hot-Plug Spec. Each platform vendor is permitted to tailor the Hot-Plug Controller to fit specific product requirements. For example, the platform vendor could trade cost and complexity between the Hot-Plug Controller and its device driver (the Hot-Plug System Driver). At one extreme the Hot-Plug Controller hardware could be simplified to a set of I/O bits that directly control each set of bus isolation devices, and each slot power switch. In that case all sequencing and timing requirements would be fulfilled by the Hot-Plug System Driver. At the other extreme the Hot-Plug System Driver software could be simplified to use a single I/O bit to control the state of each slot. In that case the Hot-Plug Controller would be responsible for fulfilling the sequencing and timing requirements.

17

Hot-Plug Primitives

The set of requests issued by the Hot-Plug Service to the Hot-Plug System Driver to control hot-plug slots or to determine their status. There are four hot-plug primitives:

- Querying the Hot-Plug System Driver
- Setting Slot Status
- Querying Slot Status
- Asynchronous Notification of Slot Status Change

The hot-plug primitives constitute the interface between application-level hot-plug software (the Hot-Plug Service) and device-driver-level hot-plug software (the Hot-Plug System Driver). However, since each operating system uses radically different device driver models, the primitive interface is completely generic. The primitives define the kinds of information that must be passed back and forth across the interface to manage hot-plug slots. Detailed specification of this software interface is left to the individual operating system vendors. These details include such things as the exact encodings of the requests and their parameters, and procedural error conditions such as "invalid parameter." Furthermore, the operating system vendor is permitted to combine or split the primitives into as many actual driver requests as are appropriate for his environment. Section 5.7. presents a detailed discussion of the primitives.

Hot-Plug Service

This term describes a broad collection of software routines, supplied by the operating system vendor, that control high-level hot-plug operations. It is only loosely defined in the Hot-Plug Spec, because the definition of most of the high-level hot-plug functions is assigned to the operating system vendor.

The Hot-Plug Service includes the hot-plug user interface. The user issues commands to turn slots on and off, and receives information about the status of slots through this interface. Most implementations of the Hot-Plug Service will also include an interface for remotely issuing the same commands, and receiving the same status as the direct user interface. This is illustrated in Figure 2-1 by an application programming interface (API) to a Management Agent.

The Hot-Plug Service is responsible for overall control of hot-plug operations. It controls the sequence of interactions with the adapter driver and the Hot-Plug System Driver to guarantee graceful quiescing of adapter activity before a hot-removal. It similarly controls the interactions with the Hot-Plug System Driver, the Platform Configuration Routine, and the adapter driver to gracefully turn on a slot and start using the card after a hot-insertion.

Hot-Plug System Driver

The device driver responsible for the Hot-Plug Controller. It is supplied by the platform vendor, who makes trade-offs between the complexity of the Hot-Plug System Driver and the Hot-Plug Controller. See Hot-Plug Controller above for more details.

Management Agent

System management routines capable of performing hot-plug operations from a remote location. See Hot-Plug Service for more details.

Operating System
A term used loosely in this context to include all the rest of the system software not specifically detailed in Figure 2-1.

PCI Bus
A bus compliant to the PCI 2.0 or 2.1 specifications, in any of the various signaling levels, bus widths, and frequencies. These include:
- 5 V and 3.3 V signaling.
- 32-bit and 64-bit widths.
- 33 MHz and 66 MHz frequencies.

PCI Arbiter
PCI bus arbiter. A typical implementation of the Hot-Plug Controller will require access to the PCI bus arbiter to guarantee that the bus is idle when changes are occurring at a hot-plug slot. The ideal implementation of the PCI arbiter in a hot-plug system would permit the Hot-Plug Controller to acquire the bus and hold it without ever running a transaction. Alternatively, the Hot-Plug Controller can be designed to work with a standard PCI arbiter if the Hot-Plug Controller generates a "dummy" transaction to keep the bus occupied. See Section 3.3 for more details.

Platform Core
A term used loosely in this context to include all the rest of the hardware not specifically detailed in Figure 2-1. Includes CPU(s), main memory, bridge to the PCI bus, standard system peripherals, etc.

**Power and
Bus Switches**

Each PCI hot-plug slot must connect to the system power supply through slot-specific power switches. Adapter cards are limited to a maximum load and decoupling capacitance on each supply voltage. Platforms must guarantee that the supply voltage rises at a rate between a specified minimum and maximum slew rate. See Section 3.6 for details.

Each PCI hot-plug slot must also connect to the PCI bus though slot-specific bus switches. The Hot-Plug Spec does not define the type of device that must be used for slot isolation. The simplest implementation uses transfer gates, commonly known as "FET switches," or "bus switches," or "zero-delay buffers." Each transfer gate is a single field effect transistor (FET) placed between a single PCI bus signal and a single PCI connector pin. When the FET is turned on, it behaves similar to a 5 Ω resistor. When the FET is turned off, it behaves similar to a 1 MΩ resistor. Other alternatives for isolation devices are discussed in Section 3.1.

Slot

A location designed to accept a PCI adapter card. A hot-plug system must have at least one hot-plug slot, but can have conventional slots as well. PCI hot-plug slots use the same kinds of connectors as conventional PCI slots.

Isolation devices associated with each hot-plug slot enable the signals to be isolated and power to be removed, so adapter cards can be inserted and removed.

An attention indicator must also be associated with each slot, so software can call the user's attention to a particular hot-plug slot.

PCI hot-plug slots generally require wider spacing between slots than conventional slots, to allow room for insulators between cards, or for handling one card without disturbing its neighbors.

User   System administrator or maintenance technician who initiates a hot-plug operation. The first step of a hot-removal operation *must* be for the user to inform the Hot-Plug Service of the need for hot-removal, so the Hot-Plug Service can quiesce the appropriate adapter activity. Actual removal of the adapter card cannot take place until the Hot-Plug Service informs the user that the system is ready.

After hot-insertion and the appropriate cables are connected to the adapter card, the user informs the Hot-Plug Service that the adapter card is ready. The Hot-Plug Service then controls turning the slot on, configuring the card, loading adapter drivers, and enabling the card for use by the operating system and application software.

2.2 Sequence of Steps for Hot-Removal

Many of the steps involved in hot-removal take place within the operating system and the Hot-Plug Service. Since both of these components are supplied by the operating system vendor, and must conform to the basic structure of the operating system, the actual sequence of steps for hot-removal may vary from one operating system to another. However, most operating system vendors will implement a sequence similar to the following:

1. The user determines that an adapter card must be removed or replaced, and notifies the Hot-Plug Service of his desire to remove the card from the slot.

    CAUTION: The first step of every hot-removal must be informing the software (Hot-Plug Service) that the removal is about to happen. This enables the Hot-Plug Service gracefully to quiesce adapter activity before the card is removed. The card can only be removed after the Hot-Plug Service notifies the user that adapter activity has been quiesced.

    A variety of notification methods are possible. No single implementation is required by the Hot-Plug Spec. Possible implementations include the following:

- Typing a command at the console or pressing a virtual button in a graphical user interface. This is the simplest and most cost-effective technique.

- Activating a switch designed for this purpose. This alternative requires that the platform include a switch with each hot-plug slot. When activated, the switch interrupts the software.

The second alternative is more expensive than the console alternative, but has some ergonomic advantages in cases where the user knows which physical card he needs to remove. For example the user may have followed a cable from some external location to the slot of interest. If the user knows physically which card he wants to remove, the probability of selecting the wrong card is reduced when a switch is located close to that card. However, this alternative is less attractive if selection of the card was originally made by viewing status information at the console or user interface, rather than viewing the physical slots. In that case a console operations would have a lower probability of user error.

2. The Hot-Plug Service uses operating system functions to quiesce the appropriate adapter activity. The implementation of this step is controlled exclusively by the operating system vendor to conform to the structure of his operating system. It generally includes the following steps:

   - Hot-Plug Service notifies the adapter driver to quiesce.

   - Adapter driver completes or terminates any incomplete operations. Depending upon the state of the driver and the adapter card, this could require executing bus transactions to the adapter card.

   - Adapter driver puts the adapter card into a state in which it will not initiate any PCI activity. Depending upon the design and the present state of the adapter card, this could include executing a device specific reset command, disabling the adapter's interrupt output, or resetting the devices Bus Master Enable bit in its Configuration Space header.

   - Adapter driver puts itself into a state in which it will not initiate any PCI activity. This state is highly dependent upon the design of the adapter driver and the operating system.

Quiescing adapter activity is discussed in more detail in Section 5.3.

3. The Hot-Plug Service issues a Hot-Plug Primitive to the Hot-Plug System Driver to turn off the appropriate slot. The detailed implementation of the Hot-Plug Primitive messages is specified by the operating system vendor. However, the message content in this case is "turn off this slot."

4. The Hot-Plug System Driver uses the Hot-Plug Controller to assert RST# to the slot, isolate the slot from the rest of the bus, and remove power from the slot. See Section 3.4 for a detailed description of this process.

5. The Hot-Plug Service reports to the user that the slot is off.

6. The user removes the adapter card. The card can be removed only after the software reports that all adapter activity has been quiesced, and the slot is off.

2.3 Sequence of Steps for Hot-Insertion

Many of the steps involved in a hot-insertion take place within the operating system and the Hot-Plug Service. Since both of these components are supplied by the operating system vendor, and must conform to the basic structure of the operating system, the actual sequence of steps for a hot-insertion may vary from one operating system to another. However, most operating system vendors will implement a sequence similar to the following:

> **CAUTION: Cards can only be inserted into slots that have previously been turned off by some operation established by the system designer. The Hot-Plug Spec does not define this operation. The implementation may vary from one system to another. The most elaborate systems might implement protection mechanisms that automatically turn off a slot before a card can be inserted. The most cost-sensitive systems might not enforce the rule at all, and trust the user to notify the software to turn off the slot before he inserts the card. See Chapter 7 for an example of one platform implementation.**

1. The slot is turned off by the method established by the system designer.

2. The user inserts the new adapter card and connects any external cables.

3. The user notifies the Hot-Plug Service to turn on the slot containing the new adapter card. The preferred form of notification is an entry on the console. Even if the platform implements switches for notification of hot-removal, a console entry is still preferred for notification of hot-insertion. In many cases the new adapter card cannot be powered-on successfully until external cables have been attached, or remote devices such as disk drive chassis have been turned on. Console operations can prompt the user to verify that everything is really ready before turning on the slot.

4. The Hot-Plug Service issues a Hot-Plug Primitive to the Hot-Plug System Driver to turn on the appropriate slot. The detailed implementation of the Hot-Plug Primitive messages is specified by the operating system vendor. However, the message content in this case is "turn on this slot."

5. The Hot-Plug System Driver uses the Hot-Plug Controller to power-on the slot, deassert RST# to the slot, and connect the slot to the bus. See Section 3.5 for a detailed description of this process. Some operating system vendors will specify that the Hot-Plug System Driver must also initialize the card's Configuration Space header, and assign whatever system resources (memory and I/O address, etc.) it requires.

6. The Hot-Plug Service notifies the operating system that the new adapter card is installed. The operating system is required to do the following:

    • Initialize the adapter card's Configuration Space header and assign whatever system resources (memory and I/O address, etc.) it requires (for those operating systems, which do not require the Hot-Plug System Driver to perform this operation in Step 5).

    • Make the appropriate adapter driver ready to use the new device.

    • Complete the initialization of the adapter card by calling the adapter driver to initialize the card. If the card contains an option ROM that includes an Open Firmware (IEEE 1275-1994) image, then the ROM image can be executed to initialize the card.

7. The Hot-Plug Service notifies the user that the card is ready.

2.4 Backward Compatibility

A hot-plug system requires a hot-plug platform, a hot-plug operating system, and hot-plug adapter drivers. A system can include any combination of hot-plug and conventional versions of each of these components, including a mix of both hot-plug and conventional adapter drivers. However, a particular adapter card can be hot-plugged only if all three components for that card support hot-plug operation.

A hot-plug platform supports loading a conventional operating system. Before the operating system loads, the hot-plug platform turns on all adapter cards and initializes their Configuration Space header. The system behaves as a conventional system if no hot-plug software is loaded.

Hot-plug operating systems are designed to load and execute on any platform. If no Hot-Plug Controller is found on the platform, then the operating system will not permit the user to perform any hot-plug operations at the user interface.

Hot-plug operating systems generally require driver modifications to support quiescing adapter activity, and initializing a card after a hot-insertion. However, as with any driver revision, the operating system will often support previous generations of drivers. Furthermore, in some cases the new driver model is defined such that the new driver can be loaded onto the previous version of the operating system. If a conventional driver is loaded onto a hot-plug operating system, or vice versa, the driver will continue to have the same capability it always had in the conventional application. However, the adapter card cannot be hot-plugged unless both the driver and the operating system support the hot-plug operation.

3. Platform Electrical Requirements

All the electrical aspects of hot-plug operations that affect the platform are presented in this chapter. Platform requirements discussed elsewhere in this book are also duplicated in this chapter for easy reference.

3.1 Bus Isolation Alternatives

A hot-plug platform must provide a means for the Hot-Plug Controller to isolate all signal pins on a hot-plug slot from the PCI bus. The Hot-Plug Spec provides complete freedom in the implementation of this requirement. A variety of alternatives exist; some examples are shown below.

3.1.1 Transfer Gates

The simplest implementation of bus isolation devices uses transfer gates, commonly known by various names such as "bus switches," "crossbar switches," "FET switches," or "zero-delay buffers." Each transfer gate is a single field effect transistor (FET) placed between a single PCI bus signal and a single PCI connector pin. When the FET is turned on, it behaves similar to a 5 Ω resistor. When the FET is turned off, it behaves similar to a 1 MΩ resistor.

Transfer gates are available from various vendors in various configurations containing as few as four to as many as 32 gates in a single package. The packages commonly include standard TTL control inputs for switching the gates on and off. Many are available with a built-in bias feature that enables the device to bias one side of the transfer gates to a common voltage, when the transfer gates are turned off. This feature is useful in biasing the connector side of the isolation devices to the slot-power rails, when the slot is isolated from the bus.

Transfer gates are generally symmetrical (except for special features like the common bias voltage), and naturally bi-directional, so they require no direction control.

Although transfer gates have little impact on signal AC characteristics, they are not really "zero-delay" devices. The transistor's on-state resistance will slightly impede the rate at which the input capacitance of the adapter card charges and discharges. This effectively delays the signal setup to the adapter card device input. Furthermore, the cumulative effect on the bus of the additional parasitic capacitance of all of the transfer gates for all the hot-plug slots increases the signal flight time on the bus, further decreasing the setup time at the adapter card device input.

The platform designer must guarantee the AC timing requirements of PCI 2.1 at every slot, in spite of the effects of the isolation devices. Therefore, hot-plug systems will require more careful layout than conventional systems. The platform designer may need to reduce some or all of the following to compensate for the effects of the isolation devices:

- distance from the upstream bridge to the slots.
- number of embedded devices (that is, devices soldered to the system board).
- number of slots.

3.1.2 Bus Transceiver

Another alternative for isolating a hot-plug slot from the bus uses bi-directional bus transceivers. A bus transceiver receives a signal on one side and actively drives it from the other side. A direction control pin reverses the receiving and driving sides. Bus transceivers commonly include an output enable pin that puts all outputs in a high-impedance state. Bus transceivers can be designed to tolerate connection to a device that is powered-off. (Conventional output buffers might be damaged if they were connected to a device that is powered-off. The ESD protection diodes in the inputs of the powered-off device would clamp the outputs of the bus transceiver to near 0 V.)

Bus transceivers have two significant disadvantages over transfer gates. First, they introduce significantly more delay on the signal than transfer gates. The platform vendor will have to do more to reduce the size and number of loads on the bus to use transceivers than would be necessary for transfer gates. This effectively means that bus transceivers can only be used on small buses with few slots or loads.

The second disadvantage of bus transceivers is the control of the transceiver direction. In general, it is not possible to determine when a slot is sending and when it is receiving signals to or from the bus. Although each slot's GNT# could be monitored to determine when that slot contained the master, there is no way to determine when the slot is the target. Although circuits for sensing the direction of current flow would be theoretically possible, transfer gates are much more practical.

3.1.3 Bridge per Slot

Another alternative implementation for bus isolation devices would be to place a special-purpose PCI-to-PCI bridge between each hot-plug slot and the bus. The "special" features of the bridge would include special output buffers on the secondary side of the bus that allow the adapter card to be powered-off. (Conventional output buffers might be damaged if they were connected to a device that is powered-off. The ESD protection diodes in the inputs of the powered-off device would clamp the outputs of the bridge to near 0 V.)

The advantage of using a bridge per slot is that meeting signal AC electrical requirements would be simplified. The primary PCI bus would be loaded only by PCI bridges (which are lighter loads than the slots). From an electrical loading standpoint, placing a PCI bridge in front of each slot would enable the bus to support more slots (although bus bandwidth could become an issue). The bridge's secondary PCI bus would be connected only to a single slot so signal AC electrical requirements would be easily met there as well.

The disadvantages of this approach include data buffer effects and cost. PCI-to-PCI bridges generally include data buffers for storing data that originate on one side of the bridge, but are not ready to be sent to the other side, *e.g.*, buffers for posted-memory-write data, or delayed-read-completion data. The effects these buffers have on bus throughput and efficiency is complicated, and often difficult to predict. Sometimes a bridge can break what would otherwise be a highly efficient, long burst transaction into multiple, less efficient short transactions. Furthermore, when reading from a prefetchable address range like host memory, a PCI bridge will generally read ahead of the exact location requested by the master, but then will discard the data if the master stops the transaction without taking all the prefetched data. Reading data from host memory and discarding it wastes bus and memory bandwidth.

To mitigate the negative effects on bus throughput and efficiency the bridge will generally implement large buffers, and algorithms to guard against the data becoming stale. This tends to raise the complexity and cost of the bridge. If only one or two hot-plug slots are supported, then implementing a special-purpose PCI bridge per slot might be cost effective. However, if more than two slots are required, it generally will be more cost-effective to implement a single Hot-Plug Controller that controls a set of transfer gates for each slot.

3.2 Hot-Plug Controller

The Hot-Plug Spec uses the term Hot-Plug Controller to refer to the hardware that controls the hot-plug circuitry. This circuitry includes:

- slot-specific bus and power isolation devices.
- slot-specific sensors for card presence (PRSNT[1:2]# pins) and frequency capability (M66EN pin).
- slot-specific indicators (required attention indicator and optional slot state indicator).

The detailed behavior of the Hot-Plug Controller and its programming model is not defined in the Hot-Plug Spec. Each platform vendor is permitted to tailor the Hot-Plug Controller to fit specific product requirements. For example, the platform vendor could trade cost and complexity between the Hot-Plug Controller and its device driver (the Hot-Plug System Driver). At one extreme, the Hot-Plug Controller hardware could be simplified to a set of I/O bits that directly control each set of bus isolation devices, and each slot power switch. In that case all sequencing and timing requirements would be fulfilled by the Hot-Plug System Driver. At the other extreme the Hot-Plug System Driver software could be simplified to use a single I/O bit to control the state of each slot. In that case the Hot-Plug Controller would be responsible for fulfilling the sequencing and timing requirements.

A hot-plug platform may have one or more hot-plug controllers. One Hot-Plug Controller is permitted to control an unlimited number of hot-plug slots, but the platform is also permitted to divide the hot-plug slots into groups, each under the control of a different Hot-Plug Controller. Every hot-plug slot must be controlled by exactly one Hot-Plug Controller.

3.3 PCI Bus Arbitration and Hot-Plug Operations

There are several steps involved in turning on or off a PCI hot-plug slot. Some of these steps occur while the slot is isolated from the bus, so they have no effect on the bus. However, other steps have the potential for interfering with other bus traffic. For example, the operation of connecting or isolating a slot from the bus will change the electrical length and shape of the bus, which can affect signal propagation characteristics. Furthermore, connecting a signal pin that is charged to one voltage (even one that is not actively being driven) will affect a signal on the bus that is being driven to a different voltage.

The Hot-Plug Spec does not define how the Hot-Plug Controller will prevent hot-plug operations from interfering with other bus transactions. The platform vendor may tailor his implementation to specific customer needs. However, in general the simplest way to prevent interference with other bus transactions is to prevent other bus transactions from occurring concurrently with hot-plug operations. The Hot-Plug Controller can prevent bus transactions by using the PCI arbiter to grant the PCI bus to the Hot-Plug Controller, and then retaining ownership of the bus while the hot-plug operation completes.

The PCI 2.1 specification allows a great deal of latitude in the design of a PCI arbiter, particularly with respect to when the arbiter takes the bus away from one master and grants it to another. The PCI 2.1 specification permits (but does not require) the arbiter to grant the bus to a new master at any time that another master requests the bus. The new master takes possession of the bus one clock later, if the bus is idle. If the bus is not idle, the new master must wait for the last master to finish its current transaction and let the bus go idle.

The design of the Hot-Plug Controller is greatly simplified if it can retain ownership of the PCI bus as long as it needs it. Many PCI arbiter designs guarantee a minimum bus ownership time for all bus masters, often called a "minimum GNT# time." If the minimum GNT# time is long enough for a hot-plug operation to complete, the Hot-Plug Controller requires no special treatment by the arbiter. However, if the arbiter does not guarantee a minimum GNT# time for all bus masters, a simple alternative design would be for the arbiter to give a special privilege to the Hot-Plug Controller. In this alternative the arbiter leaves GNT# asserted to the Hot-Plug Controller until the Hot-Plug Controller deasserts REQ#, regardless of the state of the bus, and the states of the other master REQ# signals. Hot-plug operations occur very infrequently, so giving the Hot-Plug Controller preferential treatment causes no long-term performance problems. However, the Hot-Plug Controller must be careful not to retain the bus too long for any single hot-plug operation. Bus ownership times of 16 clocks or less are generally considered safe for any system.

If the PCI arbiter guarantees neither a minimum GNT# time, nor that GNT# will remain asserted to the Hot-Plug Controller while REQ# is asserted, then the Hot-Plug Controller has another alternative to guarantee that it retains the bus throughout the hot-plug operation. The Hot-Plug Controller must run a transaction on the bus to guarantee that the bus is not idle. This prevents another bus master from taking possession of the bus, even if GNT# is asserted to that bus master.

The transaction run by the Hot-Plug Controller must be a "safe" transaction that will not interfere with the hot-plug operation, or other devices on the bus. This book defines such a transaction as a "dummy cycle." A variety of dummy cycle designs are possible. The best designs will meet the following requirements:

- The transaction is a legal PCI transaction.
- The transaction is benign. It performs no operation. That is, it must address no device, or the addressed device must ignore it.
- The Hot-Plug Controller must actively drive all the PCI bus signals throughout the transaction to reduce susceptibility to electrical noise.
- If a newly connected device leaves the reset state in the middle of the dummy cycle, the device must not be confused by it.

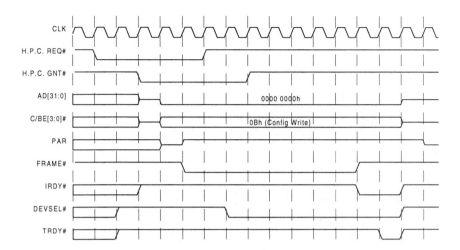

Figure 3-1: Long-FRAME# Configuration Write Dummy Cycle

Figure 3-1 illustrates one possible design for a dummy cycle. This design uses a Configuration Write command with address and data of zero. Every device on the bus would see the Configuration Write command, but since the address is zero, no device's IDSEL would be asserted; each device would assume the transaction addresses someone else.

The Hot-Plug Controller begins the transaction by pre-driving the AD[31:0] bus, as described in PCI 2.1, as soon as its GNT# is asserted by the PCI arbiter (assuming the bus is already idle). The Hot-Plug Controller asserts FRAME# for the dummy cycle one clock later. FRAME# must be asserted as early as possible to avoid the possibility that the arbiter might deassert GNT# to the Hot-Plug Controller and assert another master's GNT# before the dummy cycle started. In this example FRAME# remains asserted and IRDY# deasserted, and the C/BE[3:0]# bits are driven to 0Bh (Configuration Write) until the end of the dummy cycle. If a newly connected device were to come out of the reset state anywhere in the middle of this dummy cycle, it would observe the same transaction (a Configuration Write to someone else) and ignore the transaction.

To preserve the appearance of a normal transaction, the Hot-Plug Controller must act as the target as well as the initiator of the dummy cycle. Figure 3-1 shows the Hot-Plug Controller asserting DEVSEL# with medium timing. When the hot-plug operation is compete, and it is safe to return the bus to other bus masters, the Hot-Plug Controller deasserts FRAME# and asserts IRDY# (as the initiator), and one clock later asserts TRDY# (as the target). The transaction continues one clock later by deasserting IRDY#, TRDY#, and DEVSEL#, and floating the AD[31:0] and C/BE[3:0]# busses, and then floating IRDY#, TRDY#, and DEVSEL# one clock after that.

A disadvantage of this type of dummy cycle is the possibility of confusing the PCI interface state machines of a newly inserted device, when RST# deasserts to that slot. Typically PCI state machines are designed to begin looking for a FRAME# with the proper command and address as soon as they come out of the reset state. In a conventional system the bus is guaranteed to be idle when RST# is deasserted, because every device on the bus is being reset in unison. If a newly inserted device comes out of reset and finds FRAME# is already asserted, the results may not be predictable.

Figure 3-2 illustrates an alternative design for a dummy cycle that addresses this problem. This design is identical to the previous one except that one clock after FRAME# asserts, FRAME# deasserts and IRDY# asserts. If a newly inserted device comes out of the reset state anywhere in the middle of this dummy cycle, it will find FRAME# deasserted. Since all PCI interface state machines must remain in the idle state until they encounter a FRAME#, it is less likely that any will be confused by this dummy cycle.

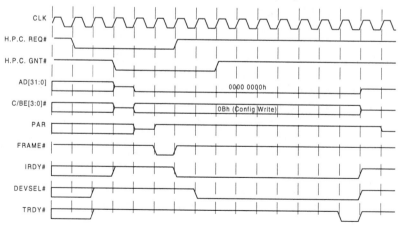

Figure 3-2: Short-FRAME# Configuration Write Dummy Cycle

The choice of the Configuration Write transaction for dummy cycles has two disadvantages related to controlling the IDSEL inputs for the devices on the bus. First, although PCI 2.1 describes in detail how the platform can connect AD[31:11] to the IDSEL input pins of devices and slots on the PCI bus, PCI 2.1 does not *require* the platform to do so. A host bridge or PCI-to-PCI bridge could assume that it (the source bridge) was the only device that would ever run Configuration transactions, and implement some method for driving the IDSEL pins which electrically isolates them from the AD[31:11] pins. If a platform does not connect IDSEL pins to the AD[31:11], the Hot-Plug Controller must control the IDSEL inputs by some other means that is appropriate for that particular platform.

Second, some platforms that do connect the IDSEL pins to AD[31:11] connect them through series resistors. PCI 2.1 describes this implementation as an alternative (although not required) to reduce the loading effect of the second device input on the AD[31:11] bus. In such platforms the initiator of a Configuration transaction is required to pre-drive the address bus before FRAME#, so that AD[31:11] have sufficient time to charge the IDSEL input pins through the series resistors. This process is similar to address stepping. As with address stepping, there is a risk that the arbiter will assert GNT# for only one clock and then deassert it, when another master requests the bus. In this case the Hot-Plug Controller would not be allowed to assert FRAME# for the dummy cycle, because the arbiter deasserted GNT# before the Hot-Plug Controller asserted FRAME#. The Hot-Plug Controller would be forced to float the AD[31:0] bus, and wait for GNT# to assert again. As with address stepping, if the bus is heavily utilized, there is no guarantee that the Hot-Plug Controller would ever be allowed to run the dummy cycle.

The Hot-Plug Controller can avoid the complications of controlling the IDSEL signals for Configuration transactions by using a memory or I/O write transaction. Figure 3-3 illustrates such a dummy cycle. FRAME# can be asserted along with the address for memory and I/O transactions on the first clock after GNT# asserts.

A memory or an I/O transaction is a safe dummy cycle only if an address can be selected that is guaranteed *not* to be assigned to another device in the system. In a PCI system, address selection can happen in one of two ways.

1. The device implements a Base Address Register (BAR) in its Configuration Space.

2. The device does all of the following:
   - It resides on the same PCI bus segment with the system subtractive decode agent (probably a bridge to a legacy bus, *e.g.*, an ISA bridge).
   - It claims an address that would otherwise be assigned to the subtractive agent.
   - It asserts DEVSEL# before the subtractive agent.

The Hot-Plug Controller can implement a dummy cycle using memory or I/O addressing only if a safe address can be selected by one of these two means. In such a system no dummy cycles would be possible until the necessary address had been assigned to the Hot-Plug Controller. If a BAR is used, then no dummy cycles would be possible until the Hot-Plug Controller's BAR had been programmed.

3.4 Hot-Removal

3.4.1 Power-Off Requirements of PCI 2.1

PCI 2.1 specifies very few requirements for removing power from a device. The requirements are shown in Figure 3-4, and Table 3-1. The supply voltages are permitted to fall in any order. If a supply voltage fails, RST# must assert within T_{fail} after the supply voltage falls below the specified limits. All PCI device outputs must float asynchronously within $T_{rst-off}$ after RST# asserts.

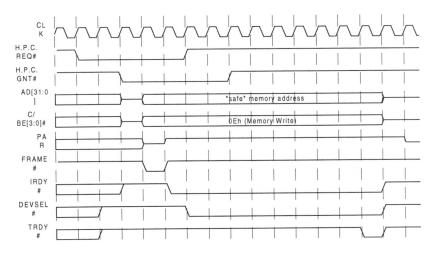

Figure 3-3: Short-FRAME# Memory Write Dummy Cycle

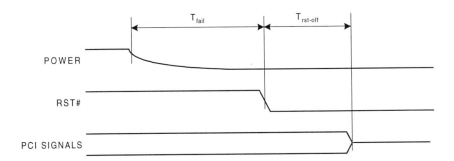

Figure 3-4: Power-Off Requirements of PCI 2.1

Symbol	Parameter	Min	Max	Units	Notes
T_{fail}	Delay between any supply exceeding its specified tolerance by more than 500 mV and RST# asserting		500	ns	1
	Delay between the 5V rail falling below the 3.3V rail by more than 300 mV and RST# asserting		100	ns	1
$T_{rst-off}$	Delay between RST# asserting and all outputs floating		40	ns	1,2

Notes
1. PCI devices must assume that RST# asserts asynchronously to CLK. The system may optionally assert RST# either synchronously or asynchronously to CLK.
2. All outputs from a PCI device are required to float asynchronously when RST# is asserted.

Table 3-1: Power-Off Requirements of PCI 2.1

3.4.2 Power-Off Requirements of PCI Hot-Plug

The Hot-Plug Spec allows a great deal of latitude for the Hot-Plug Controller to turn off a slot. No requirements are specified beyond those of PCI 2.1. However, in general the sequence of events will differ slightly from that shown in Figure 3-4. The Hot-Plug Controller generally will isolate the slot from the bus and assert RST# to the slot (in either order), and then remove power.

Figure 3-6, Figure 3-7, and Figure 3-8, illustrate various alternative sequences for turning off a slot. Each figure shows the following signals. Refer to Figure 3-5 for an explanation of the signal naming convention.

- SLOT POWER. Represents a typical supply voltage at the connector.
- PCI BUS SIGNALS. The PCI signals on the bus side of the isolation devices.
- PCI SLOT SIGNALS. The PCI signals on the slot side of the isolation devices.
- SLOT RST#. Slot-specific RST#.
- H.P.C. REQ#. PCI arbitration REQ# from the Hot-Plug Controller.
- H.P.C. GNT#. PCI arbitration GNT# to the Hot-Plug Controller.

- BUS ENABLE#. Control signal from the Hot-Plug Controller to the bus isolation devices. Low = connected.
- POWER ENABLE#. Control signal from the Hot-Plug Controller to the slot power switch. Low = power on.

The figures show the use of the Hot-Plug Controller's REQ# and GNT# signals to acquire the PCI bus from the PCI arbiter to prevent hot-plug operations from interfering with bus transactions. The figures assume the arbiter design allows special privileges to the Hot-Plug Controller as described in Section 3.3, and leaves GNT# asserted as long as REQ# is asserted. If the arbiter does not allow special privileges to the Hot-Plug Controller, the equivalent sequences could be created using dummy cycles. For simplicity the figures further assume that the bus is idle when GNT# asserts, so the Hot-Plug Controller can take possession of the bus immediately.

Figure 3-6 illustrates a typical slot-off sequence in which the Hot-Plug Controller asserts RST# to the slot before isolating the slot from the bus. The sequence begins when the Hot-Plug Controller requests the bus by asserting REQ#. When GNT# asserts, the Hot-Plug Controller takes possession of the bus. (This assumes the previous bus owner was already finished and the bus is idle, *i.e.*, FRAME# and IRDY# are both deasserted.) When the Hot-Plug Controller acquires the bus, it actively drives the bus to the idle state. (If the arbiter did not allow special privileges for the Hot-Plug Controller, the Hot-Plug Controller would drive the dummy cycle instead.) With the bus driven to the idle state, the Hot-Plug Controller asserts RST# to the slot. The device in the slot is required by PCI 2.1 to float asynchronously all of its outputs when RST# is asserted. Figure 3-6 then shows the Hot-Plug Controller deasserting REQ# and giving up the bus to other bus masters. Next the Hot-Plug Controller reasserts REQ# to acquire the bus again for switching the bus isolation devices. When the Hot-Plug Controller reacquires the bus, it drives the idle state again, and deasserts BUS ENABLE# to isolate the slot from the bus. When the slot is isolated from the bus, the system board must bias the slot signals to the same state that the Hot-Plug Controller drives when it owns the bus, thereby reducing transients on these signals. Once the slot is reset and isolated from the bus, the Hot-Plug Controller deasserts POWER ENABLE# to turn off the slot power.

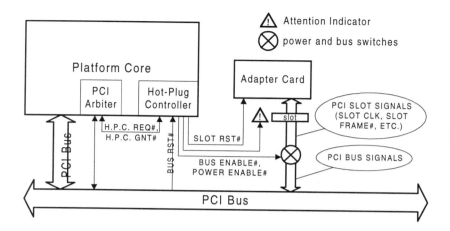

Figure 3-5: Signal Naming Conventions

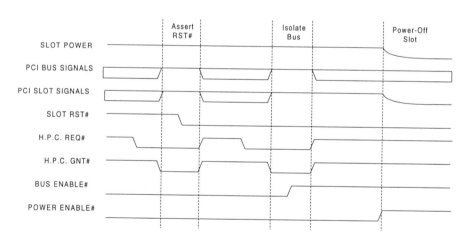

**Figure 3-6: Slot-Off Sequence Example—RST# Before Isolate
(2 GNT#)**

Figure 3-7 illustrates an alternative design of the Hot-Plug Controller that uses only one bus arbitration cycle both for asserting RST# to the slot and isolating the bus. Since there are few timing requirements related to powering-off a device, the Hot-Plug Controller has a great deal of flexibility in the power-off sequence.

Neither of these two alternatives have any significant advantages over the other.

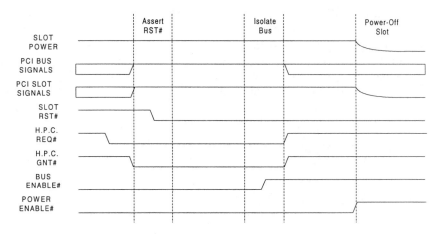

Figure 3-7: Slot-Off Sequence Example—RST# Before Isolate (1 GNT#)

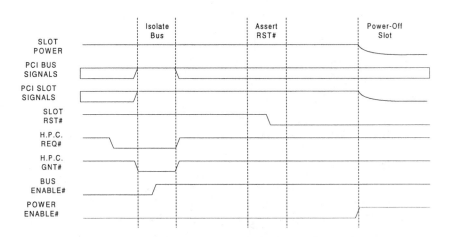

Figure 3-8: Slot-Off Sequence Example—Isolate Before RST#

Figure 3-8 illustrates another alternative for powering off a slot. It shows that the bus can be isolated before RST# is asserted to the slot. Once the slot is isolated, there is no further need to hold the bus idle while completing the power-off sequences, so only one GNT# cycle is necessary.

Unlike the alternatives in which RST# asserts first, in this case the biased state of the connector pins is critical between the times when the bus is isolated and RST# asserts to the slot. The connector pins must be biased to valid logic levels and must signal an idle bus state. Otherwise the behavior of the adapter card would be unpredictable until the slot's RST# pin asserted.

3.5 Hot-Insertion

3.5.1 Power-On Requirements of PCI 2.1

PCI 2.1 specifies several requirements related to applying power to a device, and asserting and deasserting RST#. These requirements are shown in Figure 3-9, and Table 3-2. The platform must guarantee that RST# remains asserted for at least T_{rst} after the supply voltages are stable and within tolerance. The adapter card can depend upon CLK meeting its specification for at least $T_{rst\text{-}clk}$ before RST# deasserts. However, there are no specifications for the behavior of CLK# prior to this time. Adapter cards cannot depend on CLK having any particular timing characteristics or valid logic levels prior to its setup to the rising edge of RST#.

Some examples of how CLK might behave prior to its stable setup to RST# include the following:

- CLK could remain at a logic low level continuously from the time power is first applied until the bus signals are connected, then change instantaneously to the proper frequency.

- Pulse widths might be of any value, and logic levels may not be valid.

- CLK could begin toggling between ground and the ramping supply voltage, while the supply voltage is ramping.

- CLK could oscillate at various frequencies for various periods of time, or continuously vary in frequency.

- Other examples are also possible.

In 64-bit PCI systems the state of REQ64# at the rising edge of RST# indicates to 64-bit devices whether the bus is 64-bits wide. A 64-bit platform must assert REQ64# at least T_{rrsu} before RST# deasserts, and hold it asserted T_{rrh} after RST# deasserts. In 32-bit PCI systems REQ64# is generally pulled to a high logic level with a pull-up resistor, so the setup and hold times are automatically met.

Two new parameters were added by Engineering Change Request (ECR) to the PCI 2.1 specification. They concern the delay from the time RST# deasserts until the first transactions appear on the PCI bus. The first such parameter is T_{rhff}. The bus is guaranteed to be idle for T_{rhff} after RST# deasserts. This is enough time for most PCI devices to reset their state machines and prepare to track the first transactions on the bus. Any device that requires more than T_{rhff} to reset its state machines must tolerate transactions on the bus between other devices, while it completes its internal reset. Once the internal reset is complete, such a device must wait for the PCI bus to return to the idle state before the device's state machines can leave the reset state.

To illustrate the application of this parameter, consider the example of a network controller adapter card that is not fully reset until an internal phase-locked loop (PLL) locks onto a clock supplied by the network. Suppose the process of locking to the network clock does not complete until several milliseconds after RST# deasserts. Further suppose that during the time the network controller adapter card waits for its PLL to lock, the CPU begins fetching code from the boot ROM and starts to boot the system. If the network controller is on a PCI bus segment used to access the boot ROM, then the network controller's PCI interface would be exposed to the ROM transactions as they passed. Once the PLL is locked and the network controller state machines are completely reset, the state machines must wait for the bus to become idle before looking for a transaction. Otherwise the state machines might come out of the reset state in the middle of a transaction between the host-to-PCI bridge and the boot ROM device, and react unpredictably.

The second parameter added by ECR to the PCI 2.1 specification is T_{rhfa}. Unlike T_{rhff} which is the delay to the first transaction between two other devices, T_{rhfa} is the delay from the time RST# for a particular device deasserts until the first transaction addresses that same device. In most cases the first access to a device will be a configuration read from the Platform Configuration Routine that is trying to discover what devices are present. The only exception would be for devices that have preassigned, fixed addresses. Such devices are discouraged in PCI systems (except for legacy bus bridges and the boot ROM device that are excluded from this requirement).

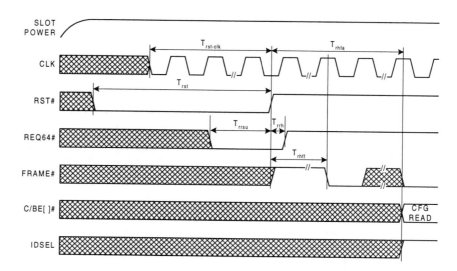

Figure 3-9: Power-On Requirements of PCI 2.1

Symbol	Parameter	Min	Max	Units	Notes
T_{rst}	RST# active time after power is stable	1		ms	1
$T_{rst-clk}$	RST# active time after CLK is stable	100		μs	1
T_{rrsu}	REQ64# setup to rising edge of RST#	10		clocks	1
T_{rrh}	REQ64# held after rising edge of RST#	0	50	ns	1
T_{rhff}	Delay from RST# high to first FRAME#	5		clocks	1
T_{rhfa}	Delay from RST# high to first access	2^{25}		clocks	1

Notes
1.   PCI devices must assume that RST# asserts asynchronously to CLK. The system may optionally assert RST# either synchronously or asynchronously to CLK.

Table 3-2: Power On Requirements of PCI 2.1

3.5.2 Power-On Requirements of PCI Hot-Plug

The Hot-Plug Spec allows a great deal of latitude for the Hot-Plug Controller in the implementation of turning on a slot. The only requirements beyond those of PCI 2.1 concern the power supply voltage ramp, and are presented in detail in Section 3.6.

Figure 3-10 through Figure 3-13 illustrates various alternative sequences for turning on a slot. Each figure shows the following signals. Refer to Figure 3-5 for an explanation of the signal naming convention.

- SLOT POWER. Represents a typical supply voltage at the connector.
- PCI BUS SIGNALS. The PCI signals on the bus side of the isolation devices.
- SLOT CLK. CLK signal on the slot side of the isolation devices.
- SLOT FRAME#. FRAME# signal on the slot side of the isolation devices.
- SLOT C/BE#. C/BE# signals on the slot side of the isolation devices.
- SLOT AD. AD signals on the slot side of the isolation devices.
- SLOT RST#. Slot-specific RST#.
- SLOT REQ64#. REQ64# signal on the slot side of the isolation devices.
- H.P.C. REQ#. PCI arbitration REQ# from the Hot-Plug Controller.
- H.P.C. GNT#. PCI arbitration GNT# to the Hot-Plug Controller.
- BUS ENABLE#. Control signal from the Hot-Plug Controller to the bus isolation devices. Low = connected.
- POWER ENABLE#. Control signal from the Hot-Plug Controller to the slot power switch. Low = power on.

The figures show the use of the Hot-Plug Controller's REQ# and GNT# signals to acquire the PCI bus from the PCI arbiter to prevent hot-plug operations from interfering with bus transactions. The figures assume the arbiter grants special privileges to the Hot-Plug Controller as described in Section 3.3, and leaves GNT# asserted as long as REQ# is asserted. If the arbiter does not grant special privileges to the Hot-Plug Controller, the equivalent sequences could be created using dummy cycles. For simplicity the figures further assume that the bus is idle when GNT# asserts, so the Hot-Plug Controller can take possession of the bus immediately.

Figure 3-10 illustrates a typical slot-on sequence in a 32-bit system in which RST# deasserts to the slot before the slot connects to the bus. The sequence begins when the Hot-Plug Controller applies power to a slot that is isolated from the bus. As the voltage rises on the power supply pins of the connector, the voltage on isolated bus signals pins (biased to the power pins) also rises (FRAME#, C/BE[3:0]#, AD[31:0], REQ64#, etc.). Once the supply voltages stabilize, the clock is enabled to the slot. Next, after waiting at least $T_{rst\text{-}clk}$, RST# deasserts to the slot.

Before the slot can be connected to the bus, the Hot-Plug Controller must acquire the PCI bus to avoid interference with other transactions on the bus. The Hot-Plug Controller requests the bus by asserting REQ#. When GNT# asserts, the Hot-Plug Controller takes possession of the bus. (This assumes the previous bus owner was already finished and the bus was idle.) When the Hot-Plug Controller acquires the bus, it turns on its output drivers, and actively drives the bus to the idle state. (If the arbiter did not grant special privileges to the Hot-Plug Controller, the Hot-Plug Controller would drive the dummy cycle instead.) With the bus driven to the idle state, the Hot-Plug Controller connects the slot to the bus. The Hot-Plug Controller then deasserts REQ# and gives up the bus to other bus masters. The Hot-Plug Controller guarantees the value of T_{rhff} by controlling the delay between the deassertion of RST# to the slot and the deassertion of REQ# after connecting the slot.

Figure 3-11 illustrates an alternative implementation of a slot-on sequence in a 32-bit system. In this alternative the slot is connected to the bus before RST# deasserts to the slot. The sequence begins when the Hot-Plug Controller applies power to a slot that is isolated from the bus. As the voltage on the power supply pins of the connector rises, the voltage on isolated bus signals pins biased to those supply pins also rises (FRAME#, C/BE[3:0]#, AD[31:0], REQ64#, etc.). Next the Hot-Plug Controller requests the bus by asserting REQ#. When GNT# asserts, the Hot-Plug Controller takes possession of the bus, and drives it to the idle state, as was discussed in the previous example.

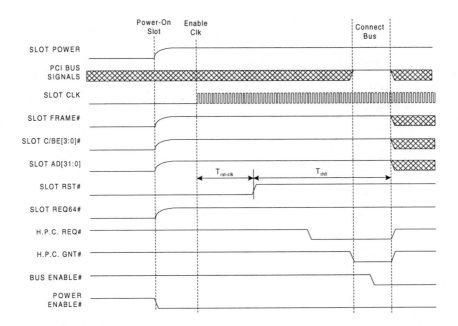

Figure 3-10: 32-bit Slot-On Sequence Example—RST# Before Connect

With the bus driven to the idle state, the Hot-Plug Controller connects the slot to the bus. In the alternative illustrated in Figure 3-11 the Hot-Plug Controller then deasserts REQ# and gives up the bus to other bus masters, and later requests it again for the next phase. The delay between these two bus ownerships guarantees the value of $T_{rst-clk}$. When the Hot-Plug Controller reacquires the bus, it drives the idle state again, deasserts RST# to the slot, and releases the bus. The Hot-Plug Controller guarantees the value of T_{rhff} by controlling the delay between the deassertion of RST# to the slot and releasing the bus.

Figure 3-12 illustrates another alternative sequence for turning on a slot. This alternative is similar to that of Figure 3-11, but combines the bus connection and deassertion of RST# to the slot into a single acquisition of the PCI bus. However, it would be detrimental to PCI bus efficiency for the Hot-Plug Controller to hold the bus in an idle state for the entire duration of $T_{rst-clk}$. Therefore, Figure 3-12 shows CLK connecting to the slot as a separate event, before the rest of the bus connects.

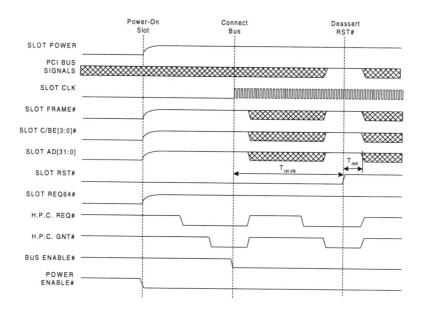

Figure 3-11: 32-bit Slot-On Sequence Example—Connect Before RST# (2 GNT#)

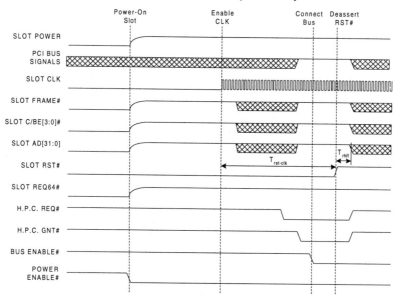

Figure 3-12: 32-bit Slot-On Sequence Example—Connect Before RST# (1 GNT#)

48

Sixty-four-bit systems introduce some additional constraints on the Hot-Plug Controller, particularly the control and electrical termination of the 64-bit extensions of the bus (AD[63:32], C/BE[7:4]#, PAR64). Sixty-four-bit adapter cards sample REQ64# at the rising edge of RST# to determine whether they are installed in a 32-bit or 64-bit slot. When installed in a 32-bit slot, the 64-bit card must terminate its own upper half of the PCI bus, since it is not connected to the platform.

Unfortunately, PCI 2.1 is not completely clear what the 64-bit card installed in a 32-bit slot should do with the upper half of the bus prior to the rising edge of RST#. In other words, what should the 64-bit card do with the upper half of the bus if REQ64# is high *while* RST# is asserted? Since there is no maximum specification on the duration of RST#, one interpretation of PCI 2.1 requires the 64-bit card to terminate its own upper-half bus whenever REQ64# is high while RST# is asserted. However, since other portions of the specification require all outputs to be disabled during RST#, the other interpretation of PCI 2.1 requires the upper half of the 64-bit card to be disabled in this case as well, and to depend upon the platform not to leave RST# asserted long enough for the devices input buffers to be damaged by the floating inputs.

REQ64# is also used during normal transactions to indicate the size of the master. To accommodate a 64-bit-card design that drives the upper half of the bus whenever REQ64# is high while RST# is asserted, the platform is precluded from using some of the alternative slot-on sequences presented for 32-bit systems. Specifically, it is not possible in a such a 64-bit system to connect a 64-bit card to the bus while RST# is asserted to the slot at the same time transactions are running on the bus. In other words, the "connect before RST#, 2 GNT#" case shown in Figure 3-11 is not appropriate for 64-bit platforms. To illustrate the problem, consider a 64-bit card installed in a 64-bit connector. The hot-insertion sequence begins with power being applied to the slot. The Hot-Plug Controller acquires the bus and connects the slot. Suppose the Hot-Plug Controller then releases the bus, without deasserting RST# to the card. Other bus masters would attempt to run transactions on the bus while the new 64-bit card was connected but held in the reset state. When REQ64# deasserts for a 64-bit transaction (REQ64# normally uses the same timing as FRAME#), the newly inserted 64-bit card would see REQ64# high while RST# was asserted. This would falsely imply to the 64-bit card that it was installed in a 32-bit connector and would cause the card to drive the upper half of the bus, which would interfere with the transaction on the bus.

Figure 3-13 illustrates additional requirements for driving REQ64# in 64-bit PCI systems. The sequence is identical to that of the 32-bit system in Figure 3-12, except for REQ64#. REQ64# is biased low before the slot is connected to bus, and is driven low by the Hot-Plug Controller along with the idle bus state, while the slot is being connected to the bus. The Hot-Plug Controller guarantees the value of T_{rrh} by controlling the delay between the deassertion of RST# to the slot and releasing the bus.

A 64-bit system could also implement an alternative power-on sequence similar to Figure 3-10, where RST# deasserts to the slot before the slot is connected.

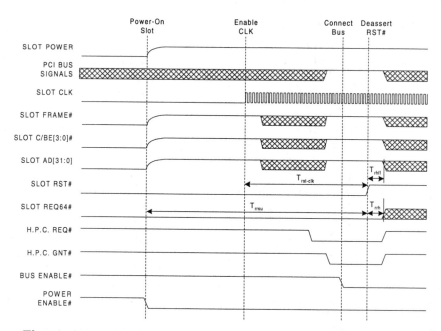

Figure 3-13: 64-bit Slot-On Sequence Example—Connect Before RST# (1 GNT#)

3.6 Slot Power and Decoupling Capacitance

3.6.1 The Specified Limits

PCI 2.1 specifies the power supply voltages and tolerances, and the maximum operating supply current that can be drawn by a slot. The Hot-Plug Spec adds requirements for minimum and maximum supply voltage slew rates, and maximum decoupling capacitance per adapter card. The combined requirements are shown in Table 3-3.

Power Supply Nominal Voltage	Power Supply Voltage Tolerance	Minimum Supply Voltage Slew Rate	Maximum Supply Voltage Slew Rate	Maximum Operating Current per Slot	Maximum Adapter Card Decoupling Capacitance
reference	PCI 2.1	Hot-Plug Spec	Hot-Plug Spec	PCI 2.1	Hot-Plug Spec
5 V	±5%	25 V/s	3300 V/s	5 A	3000 µF
3.3 V	±3%	16.5 V/s	3300 V/s	7.6 A	3000 µF
12 V	±5%	60 V/s	33000 V/s	500 mA	300 µF
-12 V	±10%	60 V/s	66000 V/s	100 mA	150 µF

Table 3-3: Slot Power Supply and Decoupling Capacitance Requirements

PCI 2.1 further specifies that adapter cards must limit their total power dissipation from all supply voltages to 25W, and must encode their maximum operating power dissipation on the PRSNT[1:2]# pins as shown in Table 3-4. Furthermore, if a card consumes more than 10W, it is recommended that the card power-on in a reduced-power state that consumes less than 10W.

PRSNT1#	PRSNT2#	Maximum Operating Power per Slot
Open	Open	0 W (No adapter card present)
Ground	Open	25 W
Open	Ground	15 W
Ground	Ground	7.5 W

Table 3-4: PCI 2.1 Operating Power Encoding

Although any single adapter card is permitted to draw up to the maximum currents specified in Table 3-3 (with a 25W limit on total power consumption), the platform is permitted to limit the maximum system current. In other words, in some cases the platform power supply will be sized less than the theoretical maximum, with the expectation that the average operating current for all the slots will be less than the theoretical maximum.

A maximum voltage slew rate for each supply voltage is specified to prevent damaging components (typically decoupling capacitors) on the adapter card by raising the supply voltage too quickly. A minimum voltage slew rate is specified for each voltage to avoid problems caused when one portion of logic on the adapter card becomes operational at a different supply voltage than another. In such cases a slow power ramp would lead to different portions of logic becoming operational at significantly different times, and possibly cause difficulty in resetting the adapter card.

Most hot-plug systems will include several hot-plug slots, so an increase in the cost of the slot-specific power switch is multiplied several times in the total system cost. Furthermore, since the slot power switches must be located near the slots, they can have considerable physical-size constraints. These two requirements typically lead to the design of the slot-specific power switches being more highly optimized to specific adapter card load characteristics than is the main power supply.

To better quantify the power supply load of the adapter card, the load is divided into two components. The first component is the transient load of charging the decoupling capacitors, and the second, "operating current," includes everything else. The slot-specific power switches are designed to charge the maximum decoupling capacitance when the slot is turned on, in addition to supplying the maximum operating current.

Although the second component of adapter card load is called "operating current," it includes all steady state as well as transient loads that are controlled by the design of the adapter card. For example, if the adapter card application has a dynamic load that increases and decreases over time, the maximum load can never exceed the maximum operating current value shown in Table 3-3. Adapter cards that include switching voltage regulators or DC-DC converters must guarantee that they never exceed the maximum current, even when charging their secondary decoupling capacitors while the slot is powering-on. The slot power switch is designed to provide no more that the operating current shown in Table 3-3, plus the transient load of charging the specified maximum decoupling capacitance.

3.6.2 Voltage Ramp Alternatives

The platform vendor is free to choose any charging characteristics that fall within the specified minimum and maximum voltage slew rate limits. A common technique is to use a voltage-follower circuit to provide a constant voltage ramp to power-on the slot. The voltage ramp must be between the minimum and maximum slew rates specified in

Table 3-3. Maximum supply current for such a circuit is derived from the operating current plus the decoupling capacitor charging current, as follows:

$$I_{max}(t) = I_{op} + C_{max} \frac{dV}{dt}$$

where

$I_{max}(t)$ = maximum supply current as a function of time
I_{op} = maximum operating current
C_{max} = maximum decoupling capacitance
$\frac{dV}{dt}$ = supply voltage slew rate.

A typical voltage waveform for a voltage follower circuit is shown in Figure 3-14. The constant slope of the voltage waveform is characteristic of the voltage-follower circuit. The figure also shows the limits for I_{max}. The exact shape of the current waveform during the ramp period cannot be predicted, because the operating current is unpredictable while the supply voltage ramps. However, the maximum value is guaranteed to be less than I_{max} as shown in the figure.

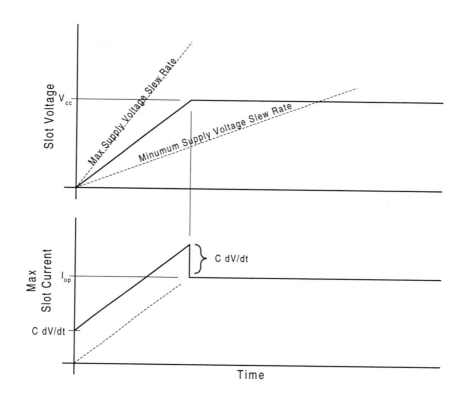

Figure 3-14: Slot Voltage and Current Ramp—Voltage Follower Circuit

An alternative design for the slot-power switch uses a constant current source when turning on the slot. In that case the voltage slew rate is derived from the current-limit value, the operating current, and the decoupling capacitance as follows:

$$\frac{dV}{dt} = \frac{I_{limit} - I_{op}}{C_{max}}$$

where

$\frac{dV}{dt}$ = supply voltage slew rate

I_{limit} = supply current limit
I_{op} = maximum operating current
C_{max} = maximum decoupling capacitance

The disadvantage of this implementation is the difficulty of guaranteeing that the voltage slew rate will remain below the specified maximum, under minimum load conditions, i.e., when the adapter card requires less than the maximum operating current and includes few decoupling capacitors. Since no minimum load conditions are specified, it is impossible to guarantee (without additional circuitry) that the voltage slew rate does not exceed the limits of Table 3-3.

3.6.3 Optional Features—Over Current Detection and System Power Budget

The slot-specific power switch may optionally include circuitry for detecting when the slot draws excessive current. The Hot-Plug Primitives include the mechanism to forward information about an over-current event to the Hot-Plug Service.

The platform vendor may optionally implement a system-wide power budget, to guard against the possibility that turning on a slot would exceed the capacity of the main power supply. In such systems the Hot-Plug System Driver is permitted to refuse to turn on a slot, if the system power budget would be exceeded. The Hot-Plug Primitives include the mechanism to forward to the Hot-Plug Service the adapter card power requirements encoded on the PRSNT[1:2]# pins. No other details for a system-wide power budget are specified. The platform vendor is free to tailor the implementation to fit the needs of the system, using whatever hardware and software components he chooses. A typical implementation would include the following:

- Knowledge of the system power supply limits, and the loads in the system. This could be supplied in tables in the system ROM.
- Software routine for comparing the present system load to the limit of the power supply. This routine must be accessible by the Hot-Plug System Driver.

3.7 66 MHz Platforms

3.7.1 Feature Requirements and Alternatives

The fundamental requirements for a 66 MHz hot-plug system are as follows:

- In 33 MHz mode, CLK may change frequency between 0 and 33 1/3 MHz at any time.
- In 66 MHz mode, CLK must be between 33 1/3 MHz and 66 2/3 MHz, and may not change frequency unless RST# is asserted.
- A slot must accept both 33 MHz and 66 MHz adapter cards, when power is first applied to the system.
- The bus must operate at 33 MHz, if at least one 33 MHz card is connected. A 33 MHz card must not be connected to a bus that is already operating at 66 MHz.
- The platform must never switch the M66EN pin of a slot without asserting RST# to that slot.

To support these fundamental requirements, a hot-plug platform must provide a minimum of the following hardware beyond what a conventional 66 MHz platform would require:

- A means for the software to determine whether the bus is currently operating at 66 MHz. The software must determine the present operating frequency of the bus to determine whether it is safe to turn on a card that is only capable of 33 MHz operation.
- A means for the software to determine the frequency capability of an adapter card without connecting a 33 MHz card to a 66 MHz bus. A 33 MHz card cannot be connected to a bus that is operating at 66 MHz. The most general implementation will enable the software to determine the state of the M66EN pin for the slot without connecting the slot to the bus, when the bus is operating at 66 MHz.

Beyond these fundamental requirements and the supporting hardware, the platform vendor determines what capabilities the platform will provide. Most of the alternatives relate to the behavior of the system when the user attempts to hot-insert a card of one frequency into a bus operating at another.

The platform is only required to switch operating frequencies of a slot capable of 66 MHz operation at one time— when the system power is initially applied. The platform designer may choose to refuse to turn on a slot containing a 33 MHz card, if the bus is operating at 66 MHz. Similarly, if the last 33 MHz card is hot-removed from a bus that contains 66 MHz devices, some platform vendors will leave the bus operating at 33 MHz until the system reboots. If this alternative is selected, the platform vendor must also decide at what frequency to initialize a bus when all the slots are empty and power is first applied. If the bus initializes at 66 MHz, then 33 MHz cards could not be hot-inserted. If the bus initializes at 33 MHz, then any card could be hot-inserted, but a 66 MHz card would operate at 33 MHz after a hot-insertion.

On the other hand, the platform is permitted to change the operating frequency of the bus at any time while RST# is asserted. Some system designs will allow a 33 MHz card to be hot-inserted into a bus with 66 MHz devices by first quiescing the 66 MHz devices, asserting RST# to all devices on the bus, switching the bus frequency to 33 MHz, and then reactivating all the slots. Similarly, such a system will allow the bus to be reset and reactivated at 66 MHz, if the last 33 MHz device is hot-removed. Because such operations affect cards other than the ones being hot-inserted or hot-removed, the Hot-Plug Service would generally need to verify that the user really understood the significance of what he was asking to do, before the operation completed.

3.7.2 The M66EN Pin and the 66 MHz Capable Status Flag

Adapter cards that are capable of 66 MHz operation identify themselves in two ways. First, they connect the M66EN pin of the PCI connector to ground through a decoupling capacitor (33 MHz cards connect it directly to ground). This allows the system to pull the signal high, if the bus is operating at 66 MHz, and low if the bus is operating at 33 MHz. Logic on the adapter card is permitted to sense the state of M66EN, so the card can change its operating mode based on the frequency of the bus. For example, the card might use a phase-locked loop at 66 MHz, and disable it at 33 MHz.

66 MHz devices also identify themselves by setting a flag bit in the Status Register in the device's Configuration Space header. If bit 5 in this register is set, the device is capable of 66 MHz operation.

The Hot-Plug System Driver must determine the frequency capability of a card to report it to the user, and to protect a 33 MHz card from connection to a 66 MHz bus. How the card's frequency capability is determined varies depending upon whether the slot is already connected to the bus. In most cases a hot-plug platform must provide a means for the software to sense the state of the M66EN pin of an adapter card *without* connecting the card to the bus. If the M66EN pin for a particular slot is low, then the Hot-Plug System Driver will refuse to connect that slot to a bus operating at

66 MHz. If M66EN is high, indicating a 66 MHz-capable card, the Hot-Plug System Driver could safely connect the card to the bus regardless of the present bus operating frequency.

In one special case, the platform is not required to provide software access to the M66EN pin state. If there are no devices on the bus other than a single hot-plug slot and the sourcing bridge, the platform designer may alternatively choose always to switch the bus to 33 MHz and connect the new card. The software could then determine the card's frequency capability by reading bit 5 in the Status registers, rather than accessing the M66EN pin. If the software determines that the card is in fact a 66 MHz card, the system can assert RST# to the special one-slot bus, switch the bus to 66 MHz, and deassert RST#.

In another case, the software must access the 66 MHz Capable flag because the M66EN pin information is not available. When a card is connected to a 33 MHz bus, the platform must drive the M66EN pin of that slot low, in case the card uses M66EN as an input. When the platform is driving M66EN low, it is not possible for the system to determine whether the card is also pulling M66EN low. In this case the software must read the state of the 66 MHz Capable flag in the Status Register to determine the frequency capability of the card.

3.8 Attention Indicator

Each PCI hot-plug slot is required to have an indicator associated with it that calls attention to the slot. Few details about the implementation of this indicator are defined in the Hot-Plug Spec, but a typical implementation would be an amber LED located close to the slot. The attention indicator is driven by the Hot-Plug Controller, with the state determined by the software. Displays on the console or a platform control panel generally do *not* meet the requirements for the attention indicator, because they are not located close to the slots, or cannot unambiguously call attention to a single slot.

Some applications may choose to combine the attention indicator with the optional slot-state indicator into a single device. To simplify such implementations the combined indicator is permitted to display only three states, slot on, slot off, and attention. For example, a single LED could be turned on to indicate the slot-on state, turned off to indicate the slot-off state, and blinked to indicate the attention state regardless of whether the slot is on or off.

The Hot-Plug Spec does not define under what conditions the attention indicator must be illuminated, but rather it assigns that responsibility to the Hot-Plug Service. A variety of applications are possible. The simplest example would be to light the attention indicator when the adapter driver detects an error condition with the adapter card. Additional user functions are also possible. For example the Hot-Plug Service might use the attention indicator to call attention to a particular slot during the hot-removal or hot-insertion operation. Alternatively the Hot-Plug Service could permit the user to determine when to light the attention indicators. For example, the Hot-Plug Service might provide a way for the user to turn on the attention indicators for all the 66 MHz slots. Or the user might designate an adapter card by its device driver and require the attention indicator be lit so he can locate a particular cable that is causing problems.

3.9 Slot Numbering

Hot-plug system hardware uses two different forms of slot identification: physical slot identifiers, and PCI bus and device numbers. (The hot-plug software also uses a third form, logical slot identifiers, presented in Section 5.6.)

The physical slot identifier is generally the slot number. It is the marking applied to the slot by the platform vendor to physically distinguish one slot from all other slots. In a system containing multiple cabinets of slots the physical slot identifier might include a chassis number and then allow slot numbers in each chassis to duplicate.

Every PCI device in a system is also identified by a PCI bus and device number. PCI Configuration transactions use bus and device numbers to uniquely address each particular device. The platform vendor assigns device numbers to devices through the wiring of the IDSEL pins for those devices, and the construction of the bridge that creates the bus. A common practice is to connect individual bits from AD [31:16] to the IDSEL inputs of each device. Decode logic in the host bridge decodes the device number and asserts exactly one of AD [31:16] during the address phase of the Configuration transaction.

Since the platform vendor assigns both the physical slot identifiers, and the PCI bus and device numbers, he is responsible for providing a means for the software to translate between the two. The platform vendor is free to choose any appropriate means for providing this translation mechanism, *e.g.*, tables in the ROM, registers in the Hot-Plug Controller, platform-specific routines in the Hot-Plug System Driver, etc. See Section 5.6 for details of slot number translation by the software.

3.10 Hot-Plug Platform Backward Compatibility

A hot-plug platform must be compatible with conventional software. If the user loads a conventional operating system on a hot-plug platform, the platform must behave as a conventional platform. If the user of that system does not attempt any hot-plug operations, the system must behave indefinitely as a conventional system.

The key to achieving this compatibility is powering-on and initializing all adapter cards the same way a conventional system would. Before loading the operating system the platform must:

- Turn on all slots containing adapter cards. This could be the hardware reset state after system power is applied, or the slots could be turned on by the boot ROM. Empty slots are not interesting, and can be left either on or off, at the option of the platform vendor.
- Initialize all adapter card Configuration Space headers.

From that time on, there would be no difference between a hot-plug and a conventional system, as long as the user does not attempt to hot-remove or hot-install an adapter card.

3.11 Summary of Supplemental Platform Hardware Requirements

The following is a summary of all the supplemental hardware that a hot-plug platform must provide:

- Slot-specific bus isolation devices. Each hot-plug slot includes devices to isolate each signal pin from the bus, while the rest of the platform is running. The isolation devices are controlled by a Hot-Plug Controller. The platform must meet all signal AC and DC electrical requirements specified in PCI 2.1, while the isolation devices are in the conducting mode. An adapter card can be removed and inserted without affecting the bus, or hurting the card, while the devices are non-conducting.

- Slot-specific power switches. Each hot-plug slot includes a switch controlled by a Hot-Plug Controller for turning off the power to the slot, while the rest of the platform is running.

- At least one Hot-Plug Controller. Every hot-plug slot must be controlled by a Hot-Plug Controller. One Hot-Plug Controller is permitted to control an unlimited number of hot-plug slots. However, the platform is also permitted to divide the hot-plug slots into groups, each under the control of a different Hot-Plug Controller.

- Slot-specific RST#. The RST# pin of each hot-plug slot must be independently controlled by a Hot-Plug Controller, while turning the slot on and off.

- A means for the software to determine the state of the PRSNT [1:2]# pins for each slot, regardless of whether the slot is on or off. The software accesses the states of the PRSNT [1:2]# pins through the Hot-Plug Controller to determine whether a card is installed or not. In some hot-plug systems, software also reports the power consumption encoded on these pins to the user, and checks the required power consumption against the available budget from the main system power supply.

- A means for the software to determine whether the bus is currently operating at 66 MHz. The software must determine the present operating frequency of the bus to determine whether it is safe to turn on a card that is capable only of 33 MHz operation.

- A means for the software to determine the state of the M66EN pin for each 66 MHz hot-plug slot without connecting the slot to a bus operating at 66 MHz. If the bus is operating at 66 MHz, the software must determine the present state of the M66EN pin for the slot without connecting the slot to the bus, to determine whether the adapter card is capable only of 33 MHz operation. A 33 MHz card cannot be connected to a bus that is operating at 66 MHz.

  In one special case the platform is not required to provide software access to the M66EN pin state. If there are no devices on the bus other than a single hot-plug slot and the sourcing bridge, the platform designer may alternatively choose always to switch the bus to 33 MHz and connect the new card. The software could then read the card's frequency capability from the Status registers, rather than accessing the M66EN pin.

- Slot-specific attention indicator. Each hot-plug slot must include an attention indicator. The location of the indicator is chosen specifically to call the attention of the user to the slot when the indicator is activated. A typical implementation would be an amber LED located close to the slot. The attention indicator is driven by the Hot-Plug Controller, with the state determined by the software. Displays on the console or a platform control panel generally do *not* meet the requirements for the attention indicator, because they are not located close to the slots, or cannot unambiguously call attention to a single slot.

- A physical slot identifier associated with each slot. Normally this is a slot number.

- A means for the software to translate between physical slot identifier (normally slot number) and the PCI bus and device number. In x86 systems this information is available in the IRQ Routing Table in the ROM.

The following is a list of all the supplementary hardware that a hot-plug platform may optionally provide:

- Slot-specific slot-state indicators. Although the attention indicator is required, the slot-state indicator is optional. The state of this indicator is implied by the state of the slot (either off or on), so the indicator requires no special software control. There is no other hardware or software in the system that depends upon the presence of a slot-state indicator, and some cost-sensitive applications may not implement it.

Alternatively, some applications may choose to combine the optional slot-state indicator with the attention indicator into a single device. To simplify such implementations the combined indicator is permitted to display only three states, slot on, slot off, and attention. For example, a single LED could be turned on to indicate the slot-on state, turned off to indicate the slot-off state, and blinked to indicate the attention state regardless of whether the slot is on or off.

- Slot-specific power fault detection. Some implementations of the slot-specific power switches will include detection circuitry for over-current conditions on the slot. However, cost-sensitive applications may choose not to implement this optional feature.

- System-wide power budget. Platform-specific software may optionally track the capacity of the system power supply and the present state of the load. If implemented, this software will compare the power requirements of each new card that is hot-inserted into the system, and, if the system power supply capacity would be exceeded, refuse to turn on the slot.

4. Adapter Card Electrical Requirements

All the electrical aspects of hot-plug operations that affect adapter cards are presented in this chapter. Adapter card requirements discussed elsewhere in this book are also duplicated in this chapter for easy reference.

One of the fundamental objectives of the Hot-Plug Spec is to enable hot-plugging standard PCI adapter cards. In theory this objective implies that there are no additional requirements for hot-plug operations beyond those of PCI 2.1. However, in practice there are certain requirements for powering-on and powering-off a single card, while the rest of the system is running, which are beyond the scope of PCI 2.1 (which assumes the whole system powers-on and powers-off together). Each of these requirements is specified in the Hot-Plug Spec in such a way as to minimize the probability that an existing PCI adapter card would not work.

4.1 Noteworthy Adapter Card Requirements of PCI 2.1

The PCI 2.1 specification includes a number of requirements that, if violated, could go unnoticed when the entire system powers-on and powers-off together. However, these requirements become critical if only a single adapter card powers-on or powers-off. This section discusses these requirements.

4.1.1 PRSNT [1:2]# Connection

Every adapter card must connect the PRSNT [1:2]# pins of its card-edge connector according to the card's maximum operating power, as shown in Table 4-1. At least one of the pins must be connected to ground. Pins not grounded must be left unconnected. PRSNT [1:2]# must not be connected to any other voltages.

Hot-plug platforms sense these pins to determine when a slot is occupied, and how much power the card requires. If the card does not connect these pins correctly, the hot-plug software could potentially not detect that the card is present, or assume the wrong value for the card's power dissipation.

If an adapter card connects an ungrounded pin to some other voltage on the card, the platform may not be able to sense the correct state of the pin when the slot power is off. For example, in a conventional system, an adapter card could erroneously connect one of PRSNT [1:2]# to Vcc. A conventional platform would always sense this pin as a high logic signal. However, if that same card was inserted in a hot-plug slot, and if the slot power was off, the platform would sense the pin as a low logic signal. The platform that implements a system-wide power budget is required to sense the pins before turning on the slot power, to verify that the system power supply can support the additional adapter card. If a PRSNT [1:2]# pin was incorrectly sensed to be low rather than high, then a 15 W or 25 W card would appear to be a 7.5 W card, and could potentially overload the system power supply when turned on.

PRSNT1#	PRSNT2#	Maximum Adapter Card Operating Power
Open	Open	0 W (No adapter card present)
Ground	Open	25 W
Open	Ground	15 W
Ground	Ground	7.5 W

Table 4-1: PRSNT[1:2]# Connections

4.1.2 All Outputs Float When RST# Is Asserted

When the RST# input signal is asserted, every adapter card must asynchronously disable (float) all of its outputs. Table 4-2 shows specifically what each output must do.

Output Type	Signals	Output Behavior During RST#
t/s or s/t/s	AD[31:0], C/BE[3:0]#, PAR, FRAME#, IRDY#, TRDY#, STOP#, LOCK#, DEVSEL#, REQ#, GNT#, PERR#, REQ64#, ACK64#	Disabled (floated)
o/d	SERR#, INTA#, INTB#, INTC#, INTD#	Deasserted (floated)
out	SBO#, SDONE	Not used by adapter cards
o/d, s/t/s	CLKRUN#	Not used by adapter cards
t/s	AD[63:32], C/BE[7:4], PAR64	Disabled (floated) if REQ64# asserted. Terminate if REQ64# deasserted. -or- Disabled (floated).

Table 4-2: Adapter Card Output Behavior During RST#

The connection between the RST# input and disabling the outputs must be asynchronous. That is, the output must disable in less than a specified delay (see Section 3.4.1) regardless of the timing of the clock, or whether or not the clock is even running.

Sixty-four-bit adapter cards sample REQ64# at the rising edge of RST# to determine whether they are installed in a 32-bit or 64-bit slot. When installed in a 32-bit slot, the 64-bit card must terminate its own upper half of the PCI bus. Unfortunately, PCI 2.1 is not completely clear what the 64-bit card should do with the upper half of the bus prior to the rising edge of RST#. In other words, what should the 64-bit card do with the upper half of the bus if REQ64# is high *while* RST# is asserted? Since there is no maximum specification on the duration of RST#, one interpretation of PCI 2.1 requires the 64-bit card to terminate its own upper-half bus whenever REQ64# is high while RST# is asserted. However, since other portions of the specification require all outputs to be disabled during RST#, the other interpretation of PCI 2.1 requires the upper half of the 64-bit card to be disabled in this case as well, and to depend upon the platform not to leave RST# asserted for more than a few hundred milliseconds.

In a conventional system, RST# is generally asserted to all devices on the PCI bus in unison. The platform central resource provides the "bus parking" feature to guarantee valid logic levels on the bus, but no other bus activity occurs. If an adapter card neglects to disable one of its outputs properly, it could cause a bus contention, but the violation might go unnoticed since the bus in not actually being used when RST# is asserted.

The platform is required to assert RST# to protect the PCI devices when either of the 5 V or 3.3 V supply voltages goes outside of the limits of the specification, or when the 5 V supply drops below the 3.3 V supply. The primary reason that PCI 2.1 requires all outputs to be disabled is to protect device outputs from damage when different power supply voltages are used by different devices on the bus, and the supplies voltages don't rise or fall at the same time. To illustrate, suppose one device, powered by 3.3 V, is actively driving the bus high. Further suppose that another device, powered by 5 V, is receiving the bus signals. If the 5 V power supply suddenly fails, the ESD diode in the 5 V device will suddenly clamp the signal to near 0 V. If the output of the 3.3 V part is not floated quickly, it could be damaged.

Although protection of outputs under unusual voltage sequencing conditions is a good reason to require all outputs to float, a violation of this specification might go unnoticed in the vast majority of systems in use today, because they use only the 5 V supply for PCI devices.

In contrast to conventional systems, the behavior of adapter card outputs while RST# is asserted is critical in hot-plug systems. In some cases a hot-plug platform will assert the RST# pin of an adapter card, and connect the rest of the pins to an active bus carrying transactions between other devices. All adapter card outputs (except the 64-bit extensions noted earlier) must be disabled to avoid interfering with the transactions on the bus.

4.1.3 PCI Interface State Machine Response to RST#

When a device's RST# input asserts, the device is required to enter the reset state defined by PCI 2.1. While RST# remains asserted, the device must remain in the reset state.

In a conventional system, RST# is generally asserted to all devices on the PCI bus in unison, and the bus is driven to an idle state by the central resource. If a device's state machines erroneously implemented a transient reset state, and then stopped monitoring the RST# input, the violation might go unnoticed because the bus is always idle.

However, in some cases a hot-plug platform will assert the RST# pin to a slot and connect the rest of the pins to an active bus carrying transactions between other devices. The adapter card state machines must remain in the reset state while the RST# pin remains asserted, regardless of the states of the other PCI control signals.

4.1.4 Behavior of CLK Prior to the Rising Edge of RST#

PCI 2.1 requires the platform to provide a stable clock to the adapter card for at least a specified minimum period of time before the rising edge of RST# (see Section 3.5.1). There are no specifications for the behavior of CLK prior to this time.

When power is initially applied to a system, in many implementations the CLK oscillator will begin functioning soon after, or even while, the supply voltages are rising for the entire platform. In many cases the behavior of CLK will be erratic while the clock generator settles to the proper frequency. Once the supply voltages are valid, CLK generally will have valid logic levels, and generally will be stable much longer than the specified minimum time before RST# deasserts. However, even though such behavior of CLK is common, platforms actually have a great deal of latitude in this area. There are no specifications for the behavior of CLK prior to its setup to the rising edge of RST#. During this unspecified time various behaviors are possible, while a slot is turning on.

In most hot-plug platform implementations the oscillator sourcing CLK will stabilize when the system was originally started, so the frequency of the CLK pin will not vary. But there may be wide variations in when the driver of CLK connects to the slot. Various implementations could start CLK as early as during the slot power-on voltage ramp, or as late as the specified minimum setup to the rising edge of RST#.

At the first extreme, CLK could connect to the slot and begin toggling as the slot power voltage begins to rise. In that case CLK would toggle between ground and the ramping power supply voltage, and be stable from the time the supply voltages stabilized until the rising edge of RST#. In other words, CLK would be stable for the longer value of T_{rst}, rather than the shorter value of $T_{rst-clk}$ (see Section 3.5.1). If CLK connects to the slot while the power is ramping, the platform design must guarantee that the logic level of

CLK never exceeds the ramping supply voltage. This generally means that the CLK output must be powered by the slot-specific power switch.

At the other extreme, CLK could connect to the slot at the last possible moment to meet the setup time to the rising edge of RST#. In that case, the CLK input signal to the slot would remain low throughout the time the supply voltage was ramping, then suddenly switch to the right frequency at the right logic levels. Several other versions of this concept are also possible, depending upon when the rest of the bus signals connect to the slot. One version would connect all of the bus signals to the slot at the same time as CLK to minimize the number of control events in the slot-on sequence. Other versions would connect the rest of the bus either before or after CLK, since only CLK (and REQ64#) have any setup time requirements with respect to the rising edge of RST#.

Adapter card designs must make no assumptions about the behavior of CLK other than its stable setup $T_{rst\text{-}clk}$ before the rising edge of RST#. All device initialization that is dependent upon CLK must complete within $T_{rst\text{-}clk}$, or complete after RST# deasserts.

4.1.5 Preference for Memory Space Rather than I/O Space

PCI 2.1 highly recommends that devices map their registers into memory space and not I/O space. In standards-based server systems I/O space is limited and fragmented. Some techniques for allocating these resources in hot-plug systems will lead to further fragmentation. For example, consider a system that has hot-plug slots behind more than one bridge (either more than one host bridge or more than one PCI-to-PCI bridge). To enable each bridge to understand which transactions it should claim from its primary bus, each bridge must be programmed with the range of addresses that have been assigned to its secondary bus. If both bridges include empty hot-plug slots on their secondary side, then one technique for assigning resources for the cards that eventually will be hot-inserted into those slots is to allocate unused resources to each bridge during system initialization. When a new card is hot-inserted below the bridge, it could be assigned resources from that bridge's allocation of available addresses.

The process of dividing the unused system resources among the various bridges with hot-plug slots will further fragment the limited resources. Memory resources are much more likely to be available than I/O resources.

4.1.6 Efficient Resource Requests

PCI 2.1 permits devices requiring memory ranges to minimize the number of bits in their address range comparator by requesting a larger range of addresses than is actually required. PCI 2.1 suggests decoding to a 4 Kbyte range for devices that require less than that amount.

Resources in many hot-plug systems will be more restricted and fragmented than in conventional systems, for the reasons described in the preceding section on memory and I/O ranges. Requesting only the amount of resources that is actually needed— even decoding below the 4 Kbyte range suggested in PCI 2.1— improves the likelihood that new devices will have sufficient resources available without having to reboot the system.

4.1.7 Switching Bus Frequencies Between 33 MHz and 66 MHz

The M66EN pin of each card indicates whether the card is capable of operating at 66 MHz. Platforms capable of 66 MHz operation provide a pull-up resistor for M66EN. All 33 MHz platforms connect it to ground. Adapter cards that are *not* capable of operation above 33 MHz must connect this pin directly to ground on the card. Adapter cards that *are* capable of operation above 33 MHz must connect it through a decoupling capacitor to ground (to provide an AC return path for adjacent signal pins). M66EN must not be connected to a supply voltage.

A common implementation of the clock frequency selection circuitry for a conventional 66 MHz platform is to wire-OR M66EN from all of the slots, and connect it to the frequency control input for the clock oscillator. In such systems M66EN will be pulled high by the resistor on the platform unless it is connected to ground by a 33 MHz card installed in a slot. Since cards are only inserted and removed while the power is off in conventional systems, M66EN never changes while the power is on.

Adapter cards are permitted to use M66EN as an input for purposes such as local phase-locked loop control. PCI 2.1 requires the platform to switch M66EN only when RST# is asserted. Even though M66EN will only "switch" when the power is off in many conventional systems, the adapter card can assume only that M66EN will switch while RST# is asserted.

A hot-plug platform is not permitted to change M66EN or the 66MHz operating frequency of a card without asserting RST#. (However, PCI 2.1 allows an operating frequency of 33 MHz and below to change at any time.) If a 33 MHz card is hot-inserted into a slot operating at 66 MHz, the platform is required either to assert RST# to all other devices and switch operating frequencies, or to refuse to turn on the slot. Similarly if the last 33 MHz card is hot-removed from a bus capable of operating at 66 MHz, the platform is required either to assert RST# to all other devices and switch operating frequencies, or to leave the bus operating at 33 MHz.

If an adapter card designer were to make the erroneous assumption that a power cycle will accompany any change in the M66EN signal, the adapter card will encounter problems in certain hot-plug systems. For example, suppose such a card is operating at 66 MHz (M66EN high) in a two-hot-plug-slot system. Further suppose that the system design allows the user to change the frequency of the bus to accept slower cards. Further suppose that the user hot-inserts a 33 MHz card and issues the commands to the Hot-Plug Service to change the bus frequency to 33 MHz and turn on the new card. In this case the system would quiesce the 66 MHz adapter card activity, assert RST# to the slot, change the bus frequency and M66EN, and restart the 66 MHz card *without* a power cycle. If the adapter card depended upon a power cycle rather than RST# to initialize some aspect of its clock circuitry, that circuitry would not operate properly after this bus frequency change.

4.2 AC Specifications

Since one of the primary objectives of the Hot-Plug Spec was to enable hot-insertion and hot-removal of standard PCI adapter cards, there are no AC specifications for adapter cards beyond those of PCI 2.1. I/O buffer designs, clock timing, output delays, and input setup times all remain unchanged in hot-plug systems.

The platform design must compensate for all negative effects of hot-plug isolation devices by reducing the number of loads, or reducing the bus length, etc.

However, while the Hot-Plug Spec was being developed, it became apparent that two parameters important both to hot-plug and conventional systems were missing from PCI 2.1 in its initial release in June of 1995. These new parameters were added by ECR to PCI 2.1 concurrently with the approval of the Hot-Plug Spec. These new parameters are shown in Figure 4-1 and Table 4-2.

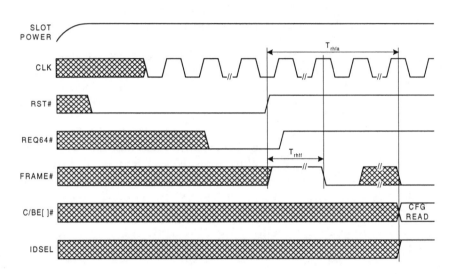

Figure 4-1: New AC Parameters of PCI 2.1

Symbol	Parameter	Min	Max	Units	Notes
T_{rhff}	Delay from RST# high to first FRAME#	5		clocks	1
T_{rhfa}	Delay from RST# high to first access	2^{25}		clocks	1

Notes
1. PCI devices must assume that RST# asserts asynchronously to CLK. The system may optionally assert RST# either synchronously or asynchronously to CLK.

Table 4-2: New AC Parameters of PCI 2.1

The first new parameter is T_{rhff}. The bus is guaranteed to be idle for T_{rhff} after RST# deasserts. This is enough time for most PCI devices to reset their state machines and prepare to track the first transactions on the bus. Any device that requires more than T_{rhff} to reset its state machines must tolerate transactions on the bus between other devices, while it completes its internal reset. Once the internal reset is complete, such a device must wait for the PCI bus to return to the idle state before the device's state machines can leave the reset state.

To illustrate the application of this parameter, consider the example of a network controller that is not fully reset until an internal phase-locked loop (PLL) locks onto a clock supplied by the network. Suppose the process of locking to the network clock does not complete until several milliseconds after RST# deasserts. Further suppose that during the time the network controller waits for its PLL to lock, the CPU begins fetching code from the boot ROM and starts to boot the system. If the network controller is on a PCI bus segment used to access the boot ROM, then the network controller's PCI interface would be exposed to the ROM transactions as they passed. Once the PLL is locked and the network controller state machines are completely reset, the state machines must wait for the bus to become idle before looking for their first transaction. Otherwise the state machines might come out of the reset state in the middle of a transaction between the host bridge and the boot ROM device, and react in unexpected ways.

The second parameter added by ECR to the PCI 2.1 specification is T_{rhfa}. Unlike T_{rhff}, which is the delay to the first transaction between two other devices, T_{rhfa} is the delay from the time RST# for a particular device deasserts until the first transaction addresses that same device. In most cases the first access to a device will be a configuration read from the Platform Configuration Routine that is trying to discover what devices are present. The only exception would be for devices that have preassigned, fixed addresses. Such devices (other than legacy bus bridges that are excluded from this requirement) are discouraged in PCI systems. The system is prohibited from accessing the new device until T_{rhfa} after RST# deasserts to that same device. The device is required to be ready for the first access by that time, although devices are encouraged to be ready as soon as possible, to enable embedded designs to initialize faster.

4.3 Slot Power and Decoupling Capacitance

PCI 2.1 specifies the power supply voltages and tolerances, and the maximum operating supply current that can be drawn by a slot. The Hot-Plug Spec adds requirements for minimum and maximum supply voltage slew rates, and maximum decoupling capacitance per adapter card. The combined requirements are shown in Table 4-4.

Power Supply Nominal Voltage	Power Supply Voltage Tolerance	Minimum Supply Voltage Slew Rate	Maximum Supply Voltage Slew Rate	Maximum Operating Current per Slot	Maximum Adapter Card Decoupling Capacitance
reference	PCI 2.1	Hot-Plug Spec	Hot-Plug Spec	PCI 2.1	Hot-Plug Spec
5 V	±5%	25 V/s	3300 V/s	5 A	3000 µF
3.3 V	±3%	16.5 V/s	3300 V/s	7.6 A	3000 µF
12 V	±5%	60 V/s	33000 V/s	500 mA	300 µF
-12 V	±10%	60 V/s	66000 V/s	100 mA	150 µF

Table 4-3: PCI 2.1 Slot Supply Voltage and Operating Current Requirements

PCI 2.1 further specifies that adapter cards must limit their power dissipation from all supply voltages to 25W, and must encode their maximum operating power dissipation on the PRSNT [1:2]# pins as shown in Table 4-5. Furthermore, if a card consumes more than 10W, it is recommended that the card initialize in a reduced-power state that consumes less than 10W.

PRSNT1#	PRSNT2#	Maximum Operating Power per Slot
Open	Open	0 W (No adapter card present)
Ground	Open	25 W
Open	Ground	15 W
Ground	Ground	7.5 W

Table 4-4: PCI 2.1 Operating Power Encoding

Although any single adapter card is permitted to draw up to the maximum currents specified in Table 4-4 (with a 25W limit on total power consumption), the platform is permitted to limit the maximum system current. In other words, in some cases the platform power supply will be sized less than the theoretical maximum, with the expectation that the average operating current for all the slots will be less than the theoretical maximum.

A maximum voltage slew rate for each supply voltage is specified to prevent damaging components (typically decoupling capacitors) on the adapter card by raising the supply voltage too quickly. A minimum voltage slew rate is specified for each voltage to avoid problems caused when one portion of logic on the adapter card becomes operational at a different supply voltage than another. In such cases a slow power ramp would lead to different portions of logic becoming operational at significantly different times, and possibly cause difficulty in resetting the card.

Most hot-plug systems will include several hot-plug slots, so an increase in the cost of the slot-specific power switch is multiplied several times in the total system cost. Furthermore, since the slot power switches must be located near the slots, they can have considerable physical size constraints. These two requirements typically lead to the design of the slot-specific power switches being more highly optimized to specific adapter card load characteristics than is the main power supply.

To better quantify the power supply load of the adapter card, the load is divided into two components. The first component is the transient load of charging the decoupling capacitors, and the second, "operating current," includes everything else. The slot-specific power switches are designed to charge the maximum decoupling capacitance when the slot is turned on, in addition to supplying the maximum operating current.

Although the second component of adapter card load is called "operating current," it includes all steady state as well as transient loads that are controlled by the design of the adapter card. For example, if the adapter card application has a dynamic load that increases and decreases over time, the maximum load can never exceed the maximum operating current value shown in Table 4-4. Adapter cards that include switching voltage regulators or DC-DC converters must guarantee that they never exceed the maximum current, even when charging their secondary decoupling capacitors while the slot is powering-on. The slot power switch is designed to provide no more that the operating current shown in Table 4-4, plus the transient load of charging the specified maximum decoupling capacitance.

4.4 System Issues

4.4.1 Remote Power Sources

Many adapter card applications include a connection to another device in a remote location. For example, a disk controller adapter card might connect to a rack of disk drives. In most of these applications the remote device includes its own power source.

Any system configuration that interconnects multiple devices with independent power sources must allow for the possibility that part of the system will be powered-on, while the rest of the system will be powered-off, indefinitely. Care must be taken to guarantee that powered devices on either end of the cable are not adversely affected by unpowered devices on the other end. For example, special cable drivers and receivers may be required, or special circuitry that detects that power has failed on the other end, and places the output drivers in a safe state.

Sneak power paths are an additional concern in remote power applications. Some designs permit some amount of power to traverse the cable from the adapter card and power portions of the remote device, even when the remote device is supposed to be powered-off. In some cases this can cause problems initializing the card or the remote device, when the remote device is powered-on. The design of the adapter card must guarantee that the card is fully reset when RST# is asserted, regardless of the state of the remote device and its power.

Both of these requirements are true of conventional as well as hot-plug systems.

4.4.2 Multiple-Card Sets

For purposes of this discussion a multiple-card set is any group of PCI cards that is normally installed and removed together. In some cases a multiple-card set is actually a single logical PCI device that simply doesn't fit on one physical PCI card. In that case only one card actually connects to the PCI bus signal pins. The rest simply connect to the PCI bus power pins. In other cases each card might appear as a separate PCI device with its own PCI Configuration Space.

Multiple-card sets introduce both hardware and software hot-plug issues. The Hot-Plug Spec describes these issues and suggests possible solutions for some. However a comprehensive solution for multiple-card sets is not specified.

The first hardware requirement for multiple-card sets is to reiterate that the PRSNT [1:2]# pins for all slots be properly connected, even if some cards in the set do not include PCI Configuration Spaces. Hot-plug platforms use the PRSNT [1:2]# pins to determine whether a card is installed. Some hot-plug platforms use the power consumption information encoded on the PRSNT [1:2]# pins to avoid overloading the system power supply. In some cases a hot-plug system will not permit the user to turn on a slot if PRSNT [1:2]# are not connected properly.

Multiple-card sets introduce other hot-plug hardware issues, if the cards in the set are electrically interconnected by some means other than the PCI bus. For example a common implementation includes a cable from the top of one card in the set to the top of another.

Hot-plug platforms are required to provide single slot control for hot-insertion and hot-removal. A platform is permitted (but not required) to provide for multiple slots to power-on and power-off in unison. Applying power to more than one slot at the same time multiplies the in-rush current that must be supplied by the platform without disturbing the rest of the system. Supplying this current generally will require larger supply connections, and more and larger reservoir capacitors close to the slots. The increased system cost of turning on multiple slots in unison, and the limited use of multiple-card sets, suggest that most hot-plug platforms will provide only single-slot control. Therefore, it is recommended that interconnected multiple-card sets be designed to tolerate having power applied to any portion of the card set, while the rest of the set is powered-off, indefinitely. This enables the user to hot-insert (and power-on) the cards one at a time. Multiple-card sets that communicate only over the PCI bus (*i.e.*, they have no side-band cables) inherently meet this requirement.

Multiple-card sets also introduce hot-plug software issues in determining exactly which slots contain cards in the same set, and locating the appropriate drivers for the set. Standard PCI configuration mechanisms do not address these problems. There is no standard mechanism to identify cards in a set.

The first problem caused by the inability of the software to identify the multiple-card set is the inability of the user to identify which slots to turn off for a hot-removal. PCI hot-plug technology requires the user to notify the software (through the user interface of the Hot-Plug Service) of his intention to remove an adapter card, and to get approval from the software before the actual removal. If the multiple-card set is physically interconnected, the user might determine which cards are in the same set by physical inspection. But no such inspection is possible if the adapter cards communicate strictly over the PCI bus. To illustrate, suppose a multiple-card set includes one each of adapter cards A and B. Each card includes a Configuration Space header complete with device ID, etc., and they communicate strictly over the PCI bus, without sideband cables. Such a multiple-card set could be installed in any slots of the system. If more than one such set were installed in the same system, there is no standard PCI configuration mechanism to determine which cards were in the same set. Without knowing exactly which cards were in which sets, the user might accidentally notify the system to turn off adapter card A from one set and adapter card B from another set.

The second problem caused by the inability of the software to identify the multiple-card set is more insidious. Suppose the user is unaware that the adapter card he wants to remove is part of a set. Without the ability for the software to recognize a multiple-card set, there is no way to guarantee that the appropriate drivers are quiesced. In the example above, suppose only adapter card A includes a device driver, and adapter card B is subordinate to card A. (The simplest example of this is when card B connects only to the power pins of the slot and connects to card A with a sideband cable. But similar cases are possible without a sideband cable.) If the user notifies the Hot-Plug Service that he wants to remove adapter card B, there is no standard mechanism for the software to discover that the driver to be quiesced is actually associated with adapter card A.

Without a comprehensive mechanism for software to identify the adapter cards of a set, designers of such sets must provide ad hoc solutions such as:

- Special-purpose software to track the multiple-card set. The adapter driver or other adapter software would ask the user which slots were associated (sideband cables case), or determine which slots were associated (individual Configuration Spaces case) and inform the user.

- User rules. Adapter card vendor develops rules for the user as to how the set is physically configured, hot-inserted, and hot-removed. For example, require that adapter card A always be installed in the slot number one less than the slot number of adapter card B, and that card A always be hot-removed first, and hot-inserted last.

- Mechanical devices that force a card set to be installed and removed as a unit.

- Combination. Some combination of the above alternatives.

- Don't hot-plug a multiple-card set. Install and remove the set only when the system power is removed.

5. Software Requirements

The Hot-Plug Spec establishes a general framework for the structure of the software of a hot-plug system, and assigns responsibilities for functions that affect more than one of the platform vendor, the operating system vendor, and the adapter vendor. However, most of the details of the software implementation are controlled by the operating system vendor, and will vary to meet the needs of each environment.

This section describes the basic requirements of the hot-plug software, and individual vendor responsibilities. Example implementations in three popular operating systems are presented in Chapter 8. Writers of adapter drivers and Hot-Plug System Drivers must refer to documentation provided by the operating system vendor for detailed implementation requirements.

5.1 Backward Compatibility

A hot-plug system requires a hot-plug platform, a hot-plug operating system, and hot-plug adapter drivers. Any combination of hot-plug and conventional versions of each of these components is permitted, including mixing both hot-plug and conventional adapter drivers. However, a particular adapter card can be hot-plugged only if all three components support hot-plug operation.

A hot-plug platform supports loading a conventional operating system. The hot-plug platform turns on all adapter cards and initializes their Configuration Space header before loading the operating system. The system behaves as a conventional system, if no hot-plug software is loaded.

In general, hot-plug operating systems are designed to load and execute on any platform. If no Hot-Plug Controller is found on the platform, the operating system will not permit the user to perform any hot-plug operations at the user interface, and the system behaves as a conventional system.

Hot-plug operating systems generally require driver modifications to support quiescing adapter activity, and initializing an adapter card after a hot-insertion. However, as with any driver revision, the operating system will often support previous generations of drivers. Furthermore, in some cases the new driver model is defined such that the new driver can be loaded under the previous version of the operating system. If a conventional driver is loaded under a hot-plug operating system, or a hot-plug driver is loaded under a conventional operating system, the driver will continue to have the same capability it always had in the conventional application. However, the adapter card cannot be hot-plugged.

5.2 Software Components

The operating system vendor, the adapter vendor, and the platform vendor each provide software components of a hot-plug system. Some operating system vendors may choose to distribute components provided by the other vendors as well as their own components.

5.2.1 The Hot-Plug Service

The Hot-Plug Service is a broad collection of software routines, supplied by the operating system vendor, which control high-level hot-plug operations. It is only loosely defined in the Hot-Plug Spec, because most of the high-level hot-plug functions are assigned to the operating system vendor to define.

The Hot-Plug Service includes the hot-plug user interface. The user issues commands to turn slots on and off, and receives information about the status of slots through this interface. The user interface is required to use physical slot identifiers (usually slot numbers) to designate particular slots for the user.

Most implementations of the Hot-Plug Service also include a system management interface. This interface enables remotely located system administrators to issue the same commands, and receive the same status as they could at the direct user interface.

The Hot-Plug Service is responsible for overall control of hot-plug operations. It controls the sequence of interactions with the adapter driver and the Hot-Plug System Driver to gracefully quiesce adapter activity before a hot-removal. It similarly controls the interactions with the Hot-Plug System Driver, the Platform Configuration Routine, and the adapter driver to gracefully turn on a slot and start using the card after a hot-insertion.

5.2.2 Adapter Driver Requirements

The operating system vendor specifies the structure of the adapter driver both for hot-plug and conventional systems. A hot-plug-ready operating system will normally require additions to adapter drivers to make them hot-plug ready. An adapter driver without such modifications would still load and operate as it always did, even with a hot-plug-ready operating system, but would not enable the adapter card to be hot-plugged.

The first additional requirement for a hot-plug-ready adapter driver is quiescing adapter activity. When the user notifies the Hot-Plug Service of his desire to remove an adapter card, the Hot-Plug Server will notify the adapter driver to quiesce activity for the appropriate adapter card. The adapter driver must do the following:

- Complete or terminate any outstanding commands to that adapter card.
- Place the adapter card in a state in which it will not initiate any activity on the PCI bus (either bus master or interrupt activity). If a software reset command exists for this device, this would be a good time to use it. The Bus Master Enable bit, and SERR# Enable bit in the Command Register in Configuration Space should be reset.
- Place itself in a state in which it will not initiate any activity on the PCI bus. If a single driver instance controls multiple adapter cards, the operation must affect only the instance associated with the adapter card being removed. The adapter driver must also remove itself from any shared interrupt chain to prevent it from erroneously accessing the quiesced device, if another device sharing the same input interrupts its driver.

A hot-plug-ready adapter driver also has two new requirements related to initializing a new adapter card after a hot-insertion. First, the adapter driver must verify that the adapter hardware is ready for use before any other operation is attempted on the adapter card.

The delay between applying power to the adapter card and initializing the adapter driver will generally be significantly less after a hot-insertion than it would be after power is initially applied to the system and the operating system loads. If the adapter card requires a long time to initialize, the adapter driver initialization routine must wait until the adapter card is ready.

Secondly, the operating system vendor may optionally require that the adapter driver replace the functionality of adapter card option ROMs after a hot-insertion. Some adapter cards include option ROMs containing machine code (for example, a ROM image of Code Type 0 for x86 code) that is executed by the boot ROM when power is initially applied to the system. In general, such machine code cannot be executed after a hot-insertion because the execution context of the boot ROM has been replaced by the context of the operating system. Although it is theoretically possible to implement a boot ROM emulation context within the operating system, most operating system vendors will require the adapter vendor to replace the functionality of the option ROM by some other means. For example, the adapter vendor could duplicate the function in the adapter driver initialization routine. Alternatively, the adapter vendor could provide an application-level routine that cooperates with the adapter driver to initialize the adapter card.

Alternatively, the operating system may support Open Firmware code segments in the option ROM (a ROM image of Code Type 1). If so, the operating system will execute the same scripts from the ROM both when power is initially applied to the system and after a hot-insertion. In that case the operating system requires no additional initialization activity from the adapter driver.

5.2.3 Hot-Plug System Driver

The Hot-Plug System Driver is the device driver for the Hot-Plug Controller. Both are supplied by the platform vendor, so the interface between them is not defined by the Hot-Plug Spec. Each platform vendor is permitted to tailor these two components to fit specific product requirements. For example, the platform vendor could trade cost and complexity between the two. At one extreme the Hot-Plug Controller could be simplified to a set of I/O bits that directly control each set of bus isolation devices, each slot power switch, etc. In that case all sequencing and timing requirements would be fulfilled by the Hot-Plug System Driver. At the other extreme, the Hot-Plug System Driver could be simplified to use a single I/O bit to control the state of each slot. In that case the Hot-Plug Controller would be responsible for fulfilling the sequencing and timing requirements.

The Hot-Plug System Driver executes requests from the Hot-Plug Service. The Hot-Plug Primitives define the interface between these two components.

Every hot-plug system must have at least one Hot-Plug System Driver. If the system includes more than one Hot-Plug Controller, the number of Hot-Plug System Drivers depends upon whether the Hot-Plug Controllers are identical, and how the operating system manages device drivers for multiple identical devices. Each hot-plug slot is controlled by exactly one Hot-Plug System Driver.

5.3 Quiescing Adapter Activity

Before an adapter card can be removed from the system, all activity to and from that card must gracefully stop. This operation is called *quiescing adapter activity*. The Hot-Plug Service quiesces adapter activity when the user notifies the Hot-Plug Service of his desire to remove an adapter card. After adapter activity has been quiesced, the adapter card will not initiate any bus master or interrupt activity, and the software will not access the card until the user notifies the Hot-Plug Service of his desire to resume use of the card.

The process of quiescing adapter activity is highly dependent upon the structure of the operating system, and will vary from one operating system to another. The process will generally follow these steps:

1. The system stops issuing new requests to the adapter driver, or notifies the adapter driver to stop accepting new ones. If a single adapter driver controls multiple instances of identical adapter cards, the driver must stop accepting new requests only for the card being removed.

2. The adapter driver completes or terminates any outstanding requests to that adapter card.

3. The adapter driver places the card in a state in which it will not initiate any activity on the PCI bus (either bus master or interrupt activity). If a software reset command exists for

this device, this would be a good time to use it. The Bus Master Enable bit, and SERR# Enable bit in the Command Register in Configuration Space should be reset.

4. The adapter driver places itself in a state in which it will not initiate any activity on the PCI bus. If a single driver instance controls multiple adapter cards, the operation must affect only the instance associated with the card being removed. The adapter driver must also remove itself from any shared interrupt chain to prevent it from erroneously accessing the quiesced device if another device sharing the same input interrupts its driver.

The operating system's implementation of quiescing adapter activity must leave the adapter driver in a state that would be appropriate if the adapter card were never reinstalled. In some environments the operating system will actually unload the adapter driver.

The operating system may optionally implement a "pause for replacement" operation, which is less drastic than a full quiesce operation, in anticipation that the same or similar adapter card will be reinstalled. In that state the adapter driver is still required not to access the card, but the driver is permitted to enqueue new requests rather than terminate them. "Pause for replacement" avoids having to return operating system resources allocated to the driver when it was installed, but must be prepared for incorrect user actions such as never reinstalling the adapter card, or reinstalling the wrong card.

One reason for hot-removing an adapter card is to replace a failed card. However, after a card fails, it may not respond properly to the adapter driver's attempts to quiesce it. It is recommended that the adapter driver detect such conditions whenever possible and use alternate means, if available, to reset the card.

5.4 Configuration Space Header Initialization

5.4.1 Platform Vendor vs. Operating System Vendor

After an adapter card is hot-inserted, the Configuration Space headers for all devices and functions (including bridges) on the card must be initialized, and system resources must be assigned to the card. The software routine responsible for managing these resources and initializing these headers is called the *Platform Configuration Routine.*

Different operating systems treat the allocation of system resources differently, and require different implementations of the Platform Configuration Routine. The operating system vendor must specify whether the Platform Configuration Routine is to be included with platform vendor software, or with operating system software.

One class of operating systems treats initialization of the Configuration Space header as a platform issue. Such an operating system depends upon the platform boot ROM to initialize these headers, when power is initially applied to the system. Generally such an operating system will depend also upon platform-vendor software to initialize these headers after an adapter card is hot-inserted. In that case the Hot-Plug System Driver (supplied by the platform vendor) will include the Platform Configuration Routine. Whenever the Hot-Plug System Driver receives a request to turn on a slot, it must not only electrically power-on the slot and connect it to the bus, but it must also execute the Platform Configuration Routine to initialize the card's Configuration Space header or headers. Since the Hot-Plug System Driver and the boot ROM are both supplied by the platform vendor, the two routines cooperate to allocate system resources.

The other class of operating systems treats allocation of system resources as an operating system function. When power is initially applied to the system, such an operating system will often initialize the Configuration Space headers with its own allocation of resources, replacing the contents initialized by the boot ROM. Such an operating system generally will specify that the header initialization after a hot-insertion is also an operating system function. In that case whenever the Hot-Plug System Driver receives a request to turn on a slot, it only needs to perform the electrical operations of powering-on, resetting, and connecting the slot. The Configuration Space header can be left in its reset state. The Hot-Plug Service (supplied by the operating system vendor) must guarantee that the Platform Configuration Routine (also supplied by the operating system vendor) is run before the adapter driver is activated.

5.4.2 Holes for Hot-Insertion

When an adapter card is hot-inserted, the Platform Configuration Routine must assign system resources to it. System resources include memory and I/O address ranges, and PCI bus numbers. Understanding the issues related to assigning system resources requires an understanding of the way address ranges and bus numbers are assigned to bridges in PCI systems.

Figure 5-1 illustrates a simple platform containing two PCI busses. Bus 0 originates with the host bridge, and includes the bridge to the ISA bus, a PCI-to-PCI bridge, two Devices A and B, and an empty Slot 1. Below the PCI-to-PCI bridge is PCI Bus 1, which includes two more Devices C and D, and a second empty Slot 2. For this discussion Devices A through D could either be on adapter cards or could be installed permanently as part of the platform.

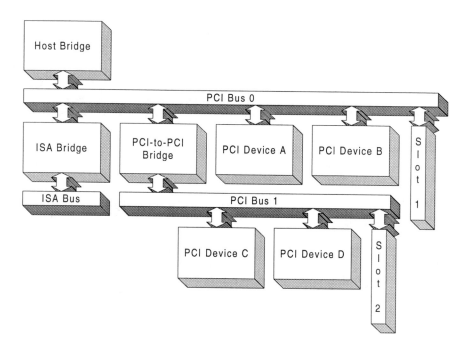

Figure 5-1: Example System with Multiple PCI Busses

Memory map (a) in Figure 5-2 illustrates one way memory addresses could be assigned to each of the devices in a conventional system. In this example memory range registers inside the PCI-to-PCI bridge would be programmed to respond to the range of addresses that includes the addresses assigned to Device C and Device D. Devices A and B would be packed next to Device D, and everything not otherwise assigned would be claimed by the subtractive decode device, the ISA bridge.

Although memory map (a) is acceptable in a conventional system, it has problems when devices are added in a hot-plug system. To illustrate this, suppose both Slots 1 and 2 are hot-plug slots. If the user attempts to hot-insert a new adapter card containing Device E into Slot 1 on PCI Bus 0, the Platform Configuration Routine can easily assign the next available address after Device B, since these addresses are not positively decoded by any device. However, if the user attempts to hot-insert a new adapter card containing Device E into Slot 2 on PCI Bus 1, no addresses are available that the PCI-to-PCI bridge will forward from Bus 0. PCI-to-PCI bridges designed according to the *PCI-to-PCI Bridge Architecture Specification*[3] have only a single range of addresses that they will forward to their secondary bus. Before a new device can be hot-inserted into Slot 2 using memory map (a), the PCI-to-PCI bridge's address range must be enlarged.

One alternative for enlarging the address range assigned to the PCI-to-PCI bridge would be for the Platform Configuration Routine to move Devices A and B when the new adapter card containing Device E is hot-inserted. This alternative has the advantage of allowing all the unused address space to be consolidated in one range. The problem with this approach, however, is the difficulty of moving devices once they are being used. If Devices A and B both used hot-plug-ready drivers, they could theoretically be quiesced and then reactivated after their respective devices were moved. This would cause the hot-insertion of Device E to have the side effect of a temporary interruption of service in Devices A and B. Furthermore, if the drivers for Devices A and B where not hot-plug ready (as might be the case if Devices A and B are soldered to the platform board, rather than on an adapter card plugged into a slot), they could not be quiesced at all.

---

[3] *PCI to PCI Bridge Architecture Specification, Revision 1.0,* April 5, 1994, PCI Special Interest Group, Portland Oregon.

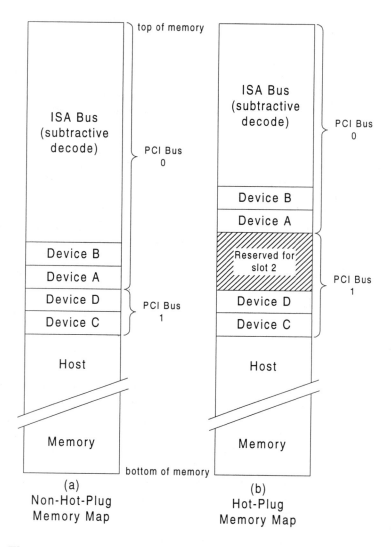

Figure 5-2: Memory Address Holes for Hot-Insertion

The preferred alternative for enlarging the address range assigned to the PCI bridge is to assign the larger range when power is first applied to the system. Memory map (b) in Figure 5-2 illustrates allocating a fraction of the unused address space to the PCI bridge for future use by its empty slot. If the reserved address space is larger than that required by Device E, an adapter card containing Device E could be hot-inserted into Slot 2 without affecting any of the other devices. The disadvantage of this alternative is that dividing the unused address space among all the bridges decreases the size of the largest hole in the address map into which a new device could be inserted. This increases the risk that an adapter card containing a device that requires a large address space could not be added without rebooting the system.

I/O address space and PCI bus number have the same allocation issues as memory address space. The preferred alternative for assigning these resources is to leave gaps for empty slots as well.

5.4.3 Partial Configuration

PCI 2.1 recommends that devices request memory space rather than I/O space. I/O address space is limited, and I/O bus cycles are often slower than memory bus cycles, since memory cycles can benefit from hardware enhancements such as prefetching reads and posting writes.

Some devices will doubly map their registers, implementing two Base Address Registers, one to request memory and the other I/O addresses. The adapter driver decides which to use. However, since I/O space is more limited than memory space, in some cases the Platform Configuration Routine will be able to assign memory resources, but not I/O resources (or vice versa).

The operating system must specify whether it is prepared to accept such partial initialization of an adapter card. Accepting the partial configuration has the disadvantage of complicating the process of starting the adapter driver. The adapter driver would have to declare whether it required both ranges or not. But by accepting a partial configuration, the operating system and adapter driver would enable the system to allow the hot-insertion of new cards even after all the I/O space was consumed or fragmented into pieces too small to use.

5.5 Controlling the Attention Indicator

Each PCI hot-plug slot is required to have an indicator associated with it that calls attention to the slot. Few details about the implementation of this indicator are defined in the Hot-Plug Spec, but the simplest implementation would be an amber LED located near the slot.

The Hot-Plug Spec does not define under what conditions the attention indicator must be illuminated, but rather it delegates that responsibility to the Hot-Plug Service. Various uses are possible. For example:

- **"Help me."** The simplest implementation is to illuminate the indicator whenever the adapter driver detects an error with the adapter card. The indicator is extinguished when the adapter driver determines that the error has been corrected, or when the card is physically removed. Generally the indicator would remain illuminated after the user notifies the Hot-Plug Service to turn off the slot, until the card is physically removed, to give the user some extra help in locating the bad card.

- **"Here I am."** A more complicated feature that the Hot-Plug Service may optionally implement is the capability for the user to specify a particular attention indicator to illuminate. This is useful in various scenarios in which the user determines which slot he wants to use by studying the console, and then needs assistance in locating the slot physically. For example, he identifies an adapter card to be removed by recognizing the name of the device or the name of the device driver from lists displayed on the console. Or he identifies an empty slot into which he wants to insert a new device, by studying on the console the number and kind of other devices already present on that PCI bus segment.

  If this optional capability is available through the Hot-Plug Service, the user can illuminate a single attention indicator to help physically find the particular slot he has picked at the console.

  The attention indicator used in this way adds an extra layer of protection against accidentally removing the wrong card.

- **"We're on."** Another possible feature that the Hot-Plug Service may optionally implement is letting the attention indicator double as a slot power state indicator. When there is no other pressing need to call attention to a particular slot, attention indicators can be illuminated for all slots that are powered.

The disadvantage of this optional use for the attention indicator is that it is confusing when combined with other single-slot uses like "Help me," or "Here I am." To call attention to a single slot, the other attention indicators must be extinguished. If the user becomes accustomed to seeing the attention indicators for all slots illuminated, he could be surprised when all but one suddenly extinguish when an error condition occurred.

Some platforms may choose to combine the required attention indicator with the optional slot state indicator into a single physical device. To simplify such implementations the combined indicator is permitted to display only three states, slot on, slot off, and attention. For example, a single LED could be turned on to indicate the slot-on state, turned off to indicate the slot-off state, and blinked to indicate the attention state regardless of whether the slot is on or off.

5.6 Slot Identification

Three different forms of slot identification are defined at various locations within the software system.

1. Physical slot identifiers.

2. PCI bus and device numbers.

3. Logical slot identifiers.

The physical slot identifier is generally the slot number. It is the marking applied to the slot by the platform vendor to physically distinguish one slot from all other slots. In a system containing multiple cabinets of slots the physical slot identifier might include a chassis number and then allow slot numbers in each chassis to duplicate.

Every PCI device in a system is also identified by a PCI bus and device number. PCI Configuration bus transactions use bus and device numbers to uniquely address a particular device. The platform vendor assigns device numbers to devices through the construction of the bridge that creates the bus, and the wiring of the IDSEL pins for those devices. A common practice is to provide decode logic in the host bridge that decodes the device number and asserts exactly one of AD [31:16], and to connect individual bits from AD [31:16] to the IDSEL inputs of each device.

The logical slot identifier is an abstraction of the concept of slot identification for use by the Hot-Plug Primitives. The Hot-Plug Primitives operate on hot-plug slots, so defining and documenting how the primitives work requires a reference to some form of slot identification. However, different operating systems use either physical slot identifiers or PCI bus and device numbers at various times. Defining the Hot-Plug Primitives using an abstract logical slot identifier avoids the need for a specific implementation in the description of the primitives. The operating system vendor defines which form of slot identification will actually be implemented in the Hot-Plug Primitives.

Since the platform vendor assigns both the physical slot identifiers, and the PCI bus and device numbers, he is responsible for providing a means for the software to translate between the two. The platform vendor is free to choose any appropriate means for providing this translation mechanism, *e.g.*, tables in the ROM, registers in the Hot-Plug Controller, platform-specific routines in the Hot-Plug System Driver, etc. The next section describes one such translation scheme.

5.6.1 The IRQ Routing Table

The simplest approach for translating between physical slot numbers and PCI bus and device numbers is through tables in the ROM. The *PCI BIOS Specification*[4] describes one such scheme for x86 systems. The layout of an "IRQ Routing Table" is defined for the "Get PCI Interrupt Routing Options" function. Although the name of the table indicates that its original purpose was to provide PCI-to-ISA interrupt routing information, the table also includes a cross reference between PCI bus and device numbers and the physical slot numbers associated with each PCI device that is physically located in a slot in the main chassis.

---

[4] *PCI BIOS Specification, Revision 2.1*, August 26, 1994, PCI Special Interest Group, Portland, Oregon.

Offset	Size	Field Description	Value
0	byte	PCI Bus Number	00h
1	byte	PCI Device Number (in upper 5 bits)	58h
2	byte	Link value for INTA#	3
3	word	IRQ bit-map for INTA#	0FFFFh
5	byte	Link value for INTB#	4
6	word	IRQ bit-map for INTB#	0FFFFh
8	byte	Link value for INTC#	3
9	word	IRQ bit-map for INTC#	0FFFFh
11	byte	Link value for INTD#	4
12	word	IRQ bit-map for INTD#	0FFFFh
14	**byte**	**Physical Slot Number**	**5**
15	byte	Reserved	0
16	byte	PCI Bus Number	00h
17	byte	PCI Device Number (in upper 5 bits)	70h
18	byte	Link value for INTA#	5
19	word	IRQ bit-map for INTA#	0FFFFh
21	byte	Link value for INTB#	6
22	word	IRQ bit-map for INTB#	0FFFFh
24	byte	Link value for INTC#	5
25	word	IRQ bit-map for INTC#	0FFFFh
27	byte	Link value for INTD#	6
28	word	IRQ bit-map for INTD#	0FFFFh
30	**byte**	**Physical Slot Number**	**6**
31	byte	Reserved	0
32.xx		*Additional PCI Device Entries*	

Table 5-1: IRQ Routing Table Example

Table 5-1 illustrates an example of a typical IRQ Routing Table containing two entries. The first entry from offset 0 to offset 15 shows that device number 11 (the decimal value of the upper five bits of offset 1) on bus 0 (offset 0) is physically located in slot 5 (offset 14). The second entry from offset 16 to offset 31 shows that device number 14 (the decimal value of the upper five bits of offset 17) on bus 0 (offset 16) is physically located in slot 6 (offset 30).

Unfortunately, no standard method is available for correlating PCI bus and device numbers with physical slot identifiers for slots in expansion chassis. Solutions to this problem have been proposed,[5] and are planned for inclusion in revision 1.1 of the *PCI*

---

[5] Autor, Jeff and Alan Goodrum, "Where Do I Plug the Cable? Solving the Logical-Physical Slot Numbering Problem," *Proceedings of PCI Spring '96 Developers' Conference and Expo*, pp. 51-60, Annabooks, San Diego, CA.

to PCI Bridge Architecuure Specification but presently have not been implemented in commercially available PCI expansion chassis.

5.6.2 Translating Slot Identifiers

The Hot-Plug Service must use physical slot identifiers in the user interface, and the Hot-Plug System Driver must use PCI bus and device numbers from time to time to run Configuration bus transactions to a devices. In between these two routines the operating system vendor specifies the encoding of the logical slot identifiers used in the Hot-Plug Primitives. Some vendors will specify the use of physical slot identifiers as logical slot identifies, and some will specify PCI bus and device numbers. This choice will determine which routines must perform the translation between the physical slot identifiers and PCI bus and device numbers.

For example, if the operating system vendor specifies that the Hot-Plug Primitives use physical slot identifiers, the Hot-Plug Service must translate nothing for the Hot-Plug Primitive. User actions on a slot are communicated directly to the Hot-Plug System Driver with the physical slot identifier. However, the Hot-Plug System Driver must translate the physical slot identifier into PCI bus and device number to run Configuration bus transactions to the adapter card (*e.g.*, to read the card's 66 MHz Capable status bit). Furthermore, depending upon whether the Platform Configuration Routine is an operating system or a platform software function, either the Hot-Plug Service or the Hot-Plug System Driver, respectively, must translate physical slot identifiers to PCI bus and device numbers to initialize the card's Configuration Space header.

On the other hand, if the operating system vendor specifies that the Hot-Plug Primitives use PCI bus and device numbers, the Hot-Plug Service must translate the physical slot identifier into the bus and device number before issuing the request to the Hot-Plug System Driver.

5.7 Hot-Plug Primitives

The Hot-Plug Primitives define the interface between the Hot-Plug Service and the Hot-Plug System Driver, by which high-level software controls hot-plug slots and determines their status. There are four hot-plug primitives:

1. Querying the Hot-Plug System Driver

2. Setting Slot Status

3. Querying Slot Status

4. Asynchronous Notification of Slot Status Change

The hot-plug primitives constitute the interface between application-level hot-plug software (the Hot-Plug Service) and device-driver-level hot-plug software (the Hot-Plug System Driver). However, since each operating system uses radically different device driver models, the Primitives are completely generic. The Primitives define the kinds of information that must be passed back and forth across the interface to manage hot-plug slots. Detailed specifications are left to the individual operating system vendors to define. These details include such things as the exact encodings of the requests and their parameters, and procedural error conditions such as "invalid parameter." Furthermore, the operating system vendor is permitted to combine or split the Primitives into as many actual driver requests as are appropriate for his environment.

The detailed definition of the Hot-Plug Primitive interface provided by the operating system vendor must also describe how the Hot-Plug Service will issue primitives to more than one Hot-Plug System Driver, in case a system has multiple, different Hot-Plug Controllers. For example the Hot-Plug Service could maintain a list of which Hot-Plug System Driver controls which slots. Alternatively, the Hot-Plug Service might broadcast each command to all Hot-Plug System Drivers, and expect that only the correct one will respond.

In the following discussion of the parameters of the Hot-Plug Primitives, a list of mutually exclusive alternative values for a particular parameter is enclosed in braces { }.

5.7.1 Querying the Hot-Plug System Driver

Parameters passed:

- none

Parameters returned:

- set of logical slot identifiers for slots controlled by this Hot-Plug System Driver

The Hot-Plug Service uses this primitive to discover the presence of hot-plug slots, and to determine which slots are controlled by which Hot-Plug System Driver. This primitive would typically be used when the operating system was starting, but can be used at any time.

The Hot-Plug System Driver must be able to report at any time which hot-plug slots it controls. The platform vendor will typically record this information somewhere in the platform hardware (or firmware), to keep the Hot-Plug System Driver portable from one platform to another. For example, the physical slot identifiers for the hot-plug slots could be stored in a table in the boot ROM, which can be read by the Hot-Plug System Driver. Alternatively they could be stored in the Hot-Plug Controller, or any other convenient location in the platform.

5.7.2 Setting Slot Status

Parameters passed:
- logical slot identifier
- new slot state: {off, on}
- new attention-indicator state: {normal, attention}

Parameters returned:
- request completion status: {
  - status change successful,
  - fault— wrong frequency,
  - fault— not enough power available,
  - fault— insufficient configuration resources,[6]
  - fault— power failure,
  - fault— general failure}

The Hot-Plug Service uses this primitive to control the state of the hot-plug slot, and the state of the Attention Indicator for the slot. The Hot-Plug Service passes the identifier for the slot, along with the new states for the slot and that slot's attention indicator.

---

[6] Applies only if the Platform Configuration Routine is executed from the Hot-Plug System Driver.

Although a hot-plug slot must pass through several intermediate states (RST# asserted or deasserted, bus isolation devices connected or isolated, power on or off), the Hot-Plug Service is required only to deal with two, slot-on and slot-off. All intermediate states are visible only to the Hot-Plug System Driver or the Hot-Plug Controller.

When the Hot-Plug System Driver receives a request to turn a slot on, it uses the Hot-Plug Controller to power-on, connect, and deassert RST# to the slot, according to the electrical requirements described in Section 3.5. After a slot is on, the Hot-Plug System Driver must guarantee that no software accesses the new adapter card too soon. Section 3.5.1 describes the parameter, T_{rhfa}, which allows all PCI devices up to 2^{25} clocks (approximately 1 second at 33 MHz) to complete their internal initialization before being accessed for the first time by the software. Generally the Hot-Plug System Driver will enforce this requirement by suspending itself for 1 second after it turns on a slot. Once that time has elapsed, the Hot-Plug System Driver executes the Platform Configuration Routine (if the operating system vendor specifies it is the job of the Hot-Plug System Driver), and notifies the Hot-Plug Service that the request has been completed. The Hot-Plug Service cannot execute the Platform Configuration Routine (if the operating system vendor specifies it is the job of the Hot-Plug Service) and start the driver for the adapter card until the slot-on request is complete.

The slot-on request returns a single parameter, which indicates whether the slot was successfully turned on, and if not, why not. If the Hot-Plug Service and the Hot-Plug Controller successfully turn the slot on, the "status change successful" completion status is returned. If the slot was not successfully turned on, one of the following failures will be indicated:

- If the adapter card is not capable of operating at 66 MHz, but the bus is presently operating at that frequency, the completion status is "fault— wrong frequency." The slot is left in the off state.

- If the platform implements the optional system power budget, and the card indicates by the connection of its PRSNT [1:2]# pins that it requires more power than is presently available in the system, the completion status is "fault— not enough power available." The slot is left in the off state.

- If the operating system specifies that the Hot-Plug System Driver is responsible for executing the Platform Configuration Routine, and if there are not enough PCI resources (memory address space, I/O address space, or PCI bus numbers) available to satisfy the requirements of the adapter card in the slot in question, the completion status is "fault— insufficient configuration resources." The operating system must specify whether the card is to be left on or off after this error is detected. Some operating systems will require the card be left on after such an error to allow the Hot-Plug Service to execute diagnostic programs, or to enable loading an adapter driver that does not need all of the resources (*e.g.*, if the adapter card doubly maps its registers into both memory and I/O address spaces, but the driver requires only one).

- If the platform implements the optional over-current detection circuitry (described in Section 3.6.3) on this slot, and if the circuitry detects that the card is drawing an excessive amount of current, the completion status is "fault— power failure." The slot is left in the off state.

- If the Hot-Plug System Driver and the Hot-Plug Controller cannot turn the slot on for any other reason, the completion status is "fault— general failure." The slot is left in the off state.

The Hot-Plug Service must accept any of the completion status indications. However, the Hot-Plug System Driver is permitted to implement a subset of the completion status indications, and report the rest as "fault— general failure." The Hot-Plug System Driver is encouraged to generate all those indications that are supported by the platform hardware.

When the Hot-Plug System Driver receives a request to turn a slot off, it uses the Hot-Plug Controller to assert RST#, isolate, and power-off the slot, according to the electrical requirements described in Section 3.4. If the system hardware and software are functioning properly, the slot-off request cannot fail, so its completion status is always "status change successful."

The Hot-Plug System Driver uses the Hot-Plug Controller to turn on or off the attention indicator as dictated by the Hot-Plug Service. The Hot-Plug System Driver and Hot-Plug Controller do not affect the state of the attention indicator in any way other than to set it according to the requests from the Hot-Plug Service.

5.7.3 Querying Slot Status

Parameters passed:

- logical slot identifier

Parameters returned:

- slot state {off, on}
- adapter card power requirement {not present, low, medium, high}
- slot frequency {33 MHz, 66 MHz}
- adapter card frequency capability {33 MHz, 66 MHz, insufficient power}

The Hot-Plug Service uses this primitive to determine the status of a hot-plug slot, and any adapter card that might be present in it. The Hot-Plug Service passes the identifier for the slot, and the request returns the slot status.

The first parameter returned by this request is the slot state. Although a hot-plug slot must pass through several intermediate states (RST# asserted or deasserted, bus isolation devices connected or isolated, power on or off), the Hot-Plug Service is required only to deal with two, slot-on and slot-off. All intermediate states are visible only to the Hot-Plug System Driver or the Hot-Plug Controller. In most cases the slot state will be whatever the Hot-Plug Service last set it to with a Setting Slot Status primitive. However, in some cases slot state will change for other reasons. (See Asynchronous Notification of Slot Status Change.)

The second parameter returned by this request indicates whether a card is installed in the slot, and if so, how much power it requires. When the Hot-Plug System Driver receives this request, it uses the Hot-Plug Controller to determine the connection of the PRSNT [1:2]# pins for the slot in question. The encoding of the PRSNT [1:2]# pins is shown in Table 4-1.

The third parameter returned by this request is the present operating frequency of the bus. The design of the Hot-Plug Controller for a 66 MHz PCI bus must enable the software to determine the present operating frequency of the bus. The Hot-Plug System Driver is required to reject a request to turn on a slot containing a 33 MHz card, if the bus is operating at 66 MHz. This parameter enables the Hot-Plug Service to determine the present operating frequency without having to turn on the slot (although the parameter is also available when the slot is on).

The fourth parameter returned by this request is the frequency capability of the adapter card installed in the slot in question. If no adapter card is present, this parameter is meaningless. If an adapter card is present, and the slot state is on, the Hot-Plug System Driver must read the 66 MHz Capable bit in the adapter card's Status Register (bit 5, offset 06h in the device's Configuration Space header). (If the slot is on and the bus is operating at 66 MHz, the Hot-Plug System Driver could assume that the card was capable of 66 MHz operation, since it would not be possible to connect a 33 MHz card to the 66 MHz bus. However, the algorithm is simplified if the Hot-Plug System Driver always checks the 66 MHz Capable bit.)

If an adapter card is present but the slot is off, the Hot-Plug System Driver will require different actions to determine the frequency capability of the card, depending upon the present operating frequency of the bus. If the bus is presently operating at 66 MHz, then the Hot-Plug System Driver must use the capabilities provided by the Hot-Plug Controller to sense the state of the M66EN pin of the slot without connecting the slot to the bus. (The new adapter card might be capable of operating only at 33 MHz, so it could not be connected to the bus to read the 66 MHz Capable bit.) If the bus is presently operating at 33 MHz, two implementations are possible. Some platforms will allow the Hot-Plug System Driver to sense the M66EN pin as before. In other platforms the original M66EN state will no longer be available when the bus is operating at 33 MHz. In those platforms the Hot-Plug System Driver must turn the slot on and read the 66 MHz Capable bit in the Status Register.

In this last case (an adapter card is present, the bus is operating at 33 MHz, and the platform design requires the 66 MHz Capable bit to be read), if the system implements the optional system power budget and the card requires more power than is presently available in the budget, turning on the slot will not be possible. In that case the Hot-Plug System Driver must indicate that there is not enough power to determine the frequency capability of the adapter card.

5.7.4 Asynchronous Notification of Slot Status Change

Parameters passed:

- logical slot identifier

In most cases the slot status will change only as a result of a request by the Hot-Plug Service. However, the following lists shows examples of situations in which the slot status changes independently of the Hot-Plug Service:

- The platform implements the optional over-current detection circuitry for a slot, and the adapter card develops an over-current fault. The over-current detection circuitry will turn the slot off.

- An adapter card is inserted into or removed from a slot that is off. The adapter power requirements will change between "not present" and the actual power requirements of the card.

The operating system vendor specifies whether the Hot-Plug Service is to be notified by the Hot-Plug System Driver when such changes in slot status occur. (The Hot-Plug Service could choose instead to poll periodically the state of the slot.) If asynchronous notification were required, the most common implementation would require the Hot-Plug Controller to detect the status change and generate an interrupt to the Hot-Plug System Driver.

The most common use for Asynchronous Notification of Slot Status Change is in keeping slot status information in the user interface up to date.

It is recommended that the automatic detection of an adapter card inserted into a slot *not* cause the slot automatically to turn on. The process of inserting a standard PCI adapter card into a standard PCI slot is sometimes a multiple-step process. The user may remove and insert the card several times before he is satisfied that it is seated properly. Furthermore, the card may require that cables be connected, or external devices be powered-on before the card is ready. It is recommended that a slot not be turned on until the user notifies the Hot-Plug Service at the user interface.

5.8 Operating System Vendor Deliverables Checklist

The operating system vendor has two kinds of deliverables for a hot-plug system: software and specifications. Furthermore, the specifications can be divided between adapter driver specifications and Hot-Plug System Driver specifications.

5.8.1 Software

- Hot-plug-ready operating system. A hot-plug-ready operating system must permit devices requiring operating system support to be inserted and removed while the operating system is running.

- Hot-Plug Service, including the user interface. The Hot-Plug Service is responsible for overall control of hot-plug operations. It controls the sequence of interactions with the adapter driver and the Hot-Plug System Driver to guarantee graceful quiescing of adapter activity before a hot-removal. It similarly controls the interactions with the Hot-Plug System Driver, the Platform Configuration Routine, and the adapter driver to gracefully turn on a card and start using it after a hot-insertion.

- Platform Configuration Routine (optional). If the operating system vendor specifies that the Platform Configuration Routine is an operating system function, the operating system vendor must supply the routine.

5.8.2 Adapter Driver Specification

- Quiesce adapter operation. The operating system vendor must specify how an adapter driver will be notified of the quiesce operation, and what it should do when notified.

- Optional pause operation. The operating system vendor must specify whether adapter drivers must support a pause operation in expectation that the same or a similar adapter card will be reinserted, and if so, how it should support this operation.

- Option ROM requirements. The operating system vendor must specify what requirements the adapter driver has with respect to option ROMs on the adapter card. Possible requirements include but are not limited to the following:

  - No requirements if the option ROM includes an Open Firmware code image. The same interpretive code is executed both when power is initially applied to the system and after a hot-insertion.

  - No requirements. The option ROM code will be executed under a synthetic boot environment created by the operating system.

- All adapter card initialization functions must be reproduced by the driver after a hot-insertion.

- Driver start operation. The operating system vendor must specify how an adapter driver will be notified to start using a newly inserted adapter card, or resume using an old one after a pause operation.

5.8.3 Hot-Plug System Driver Specification

- Hot-Plug Primitives. The operating system vendor must specify the form and structure of the Hot-Plug Primitives, including all the parameters such as the logical slot identifier.

- Platform Configuration Routine. The operating system vendor must specify whether the Hot-Plug System Driver is responsible for executing the Platform Configuration Routine.

6. Mechanical Requirements

The Hot-Plug Spec does not define any mechanical requirements for a hot-plug system other than the use of standard adapter cards as defined by PCI 2.1. The platform vendor is permitted to optimize the capabilities as well as the implementation of each platform mechanical design to meet specific customer needs.

This chapter lists some of the problems that generally must be addressed in a hot-plug platform mechanical design, and some common methods for solving those problems.

6.1 Hot-Plug Indicators

The Hot-Plug Spec defines two slot-specific indicators, the required attention indicator, and the optional slot-state indicator.

Few details about the implementation of the attention indicator are defined in the Hot-Plug Spec. The location of the indicator is chosen specifically to call the attention of the user to a particular slot when the indicator is activated. Displays on the console or a platform control panel generally do *not* meet the requirements for the attention indicator, because they are not located close to the slots, or cannot unambiguously call attention to a single slot. The simplest implementation would be an amber LED located near the slot. The exact location should be clearly visible, and clearly associated with a individual slot. Locating the LED on the system board with the slot connectors is the most cost-effective location, but in most systems is not clearly visible, and could be confusing as to which of two adjacent slots it is indicating. Locating the indicator in an unobstructed area above the adapter card is preferred.

The optional slot state indicator can be implemented either separately from the attention indicator, or the two can be combined into a single LED. The combined indicator is permitted to display only three states, slot on, slot off, and attention. For example, a single LED could be turned on to indicate the slot-on state, turned off to indicate the slot-off state, and blinked to indicate the attention state regardless of whether the slot is on or off.

Single two-color devices are available, but are not recommended for the slot state and attention indicators. A colorblind user would have difficulty determining when an attention indicator was illuminated unless there was some physical separation between the two indicators.

6.2 Protection of the User

A platform with power applied generally presents hazards to the user that are not present when the platform is powered-off. Typically these hazards are of two kinds. The first is electrical hazards. Organizations responsible for creating safety standards generally agree that voltages below a limit called Safety Extra-Low Voltage (SELV) are not considered a shock hazard to the user. DC power sources below 60 V, or AC sources below 42.4 V_{peak} (30 V_{rms} if a sine wave) are generally considered safe from shock hazard in most parts of the world. Platform vendors are required by these safety organizations to prevent the user from contacting power sources above these limits. Furthermore, some power sources at voltages less than the SELV limit are still considered hazardous if the source can supply high currents. A power source of 2 V or more is considered an energy hazard if it can supply as much as 240 VA, or stores as much as 20 Joules.

The second kind of hazard that is present only while the system is powered-on is a mechanical hazard from moving parts. The most common moving parts in most platforms are ventilation fans.

Common methods for protecting the user from electrical and mechanical hazards include insulators (for electrical hazards), fuses and other current limiting devices (for energy hazards), barriers, and interlock switches that power-off the platform when a hazardous area is opened. To hot-plug an adapter cards the user must have access to the area of the platform containing the PCI slots. The platform mechanical design must permit the user to access the PCI slots, while protecting him from hazards in the rest of the platform.

6.3 Protection of Adapter Card and Platform Electronics

6.3.1 Electrostatic Discharge

A risk of damage from electrostatic discharge (ESD) exists whenever a user comes in contact with an electronic device. The risk comes at various times during the hot-plug process.

The first risk occurs when the user contacts a loose adapter card before beginning a hot-insertion operation. Adapter cards are commonly shipped in anti-static packaging to reduce the risk of a static charge building on one portion of a card and then discharging to another during shipment. This same anti-static packaging reduces the risk of the user causing damage to a card when he first contacts it. In most cases the user will contact the anti-static package before contacting the adapter card inside, and thereby safely discharge into the packaging material rather than the electronics.

The second risk occurs when the user contacts the system either for hot-insertion or hot-removal. In many respects the ESD risks to a system that is powered-on are the same as those when the system is powered-off. Static charges in typical office environments can easily rise above 30 KV, and can destroy components just as easily when the system power is off as when it is on. The additional risk to a running system is that electrical noise induced into operating circuits by the discharge can sometimes cause transient errors. In that case even if no components are damaged, the system could crash, or cause an undetected data error.

To remove such risks the platform designer must bring the user and the system to the same electrical potential in a controlled manner. Commonly implemented solutions include:

- Grounding straps. Require the user to remain electrically connected to the platform at all times. Such devices are simple to implement and, when used, are highly effective. The disadvantage is that they depend upon the user's cooperation and discipline to wear the strap.
- Electrostatic bleeder components. Design the system chassis with exposed conductors that the user will naturally contact at the beginning of any hot-insertion or hot-removal

operation. The disadvantage of this approach is that standard PCI adapter cards and slots were not designed for this requirement, making it difficult to design effective bleeder components.

More elaborate static control measures that drain a static charge from a user through the air are also possible, but more expensive.

6.3.2 Accidental Contact to Platform and Adapter Cards

Another risk that typically effects the mechanical design of a hot-plug platform is the risk of shorting to the platform, or to an adjacent active adapter card, during the insertion and removal process. Such risks are typically avoided by insulating the electronic components from contact. The platform must be protected from the user accidentally dropping anything such as paper clips, tools, or the adapter card itself into the platform.

Furthermore, each adapter card must be protected from accidental contact with other adapter cards during the insertion and removal process. Various alternatives are possible, for example:

- Increased slot spacing. Increasing the spacing between the slots reduces the risk of shorting during insertion and removal operations.

- Insulators or spacers between slots. Locating a mechanical device between adjacent slots that prevents adapter card contact gives ideal protection against shorting one adapter card to another. However, such devices often restrict access to the adapter card, making it more difficult physically to insert and remove the card.

- Adapter card carrier. A carrier designed to enclose the card provides ideal insulation from the user and adjacent cards. However, there are several difficulties with this approach. First, PCI 2.1 permits a wide range of sizes and shapes of adapter cards. Designing an attachment scheme to secure any size card inside such an enclosure would not be easy. Secondly, acquiring such an enclosures and attaching them to every adapter card in the system would be a major inconvenience for the user. Third, any such enclosure would restrict airflow to the adapter card. A platform design that compensated for the restricted airflow around the adapter cards would be difficult and expensive.

6.3.3 Hot-Removal Procedure Violations

PCI hot-plug protocol requires the user to warn the software before any hot-removal operation. This allows the software gracefully to shut down operations on the device before the device disappears. The Hot-Plug Spec does not state how or even if this rule is enforced. Three general levels of protection are possible:

1. No protection. Rely upon the user to follow the proper procedure. This is the least expensive approach, but is vulnerable to a system crash and hardware damage if the user does not follow the proper procedure.

2. Protect the hardware. The adapter card and platform hardware are generally safe from damage as soon as the slot is powered-off. In most cases the steps required to turn off the slot electrically (assert RST# to the slot, isolate the bus, power-off the slot) require only a short period of time (a few milliseconds) relative to the time required to remove the adapter card. Hardware protection schemes can be implemented that detect when the user begins a removal operation and automatically turn off the slot to protect the hardware, if the user violates the proper removal procedure.

3. Protect the software. There are no limits to the length of time required to quiesce adapter activity. Under some extreme conditions some operating systems could require several seconds. Protecting the software from a violation of the proper removal procedure generally requires preventing the user from removing the card until the software has quiesced adapter activity. Various alternatives are possible, including the following:

    • Restricted access. Restrict physical access by the user to the adapter card until adapter activity is quiesced. This solution is analogous to a video cassette recorder in which the user cannot physically access the cassette until the recorder is ready for it to be removed.

    • Restricted removal. Physically prevent the removal of the adapter card until the adapter activity is quiesced. This approach is similar to the previous one, but is simpler to implement in the limited space surrounding the slots, requiring only an electromechanical locking device to prevent the adapter card from being removed.

6.3.4 Hot-Insertion Procedure Violations

PCI hot-plug protocol requires the system to turn off the slot before an adapter card can be inserted. But the Hot-Plug Spec does not define how this is done. Unlike hot-removal, there is no requirement to quiesce software operations before a hot-insertion, so only two general levels of protection are possible:

1. No protection. Rely upon the user to follow the proper procedure. This is the least expensive approach, but is vulnerable to hardware damage if the user does not follow the proper procedure.

2. Protect the hardware. The adapter card and platform hardware are generally safe from damage as soon as the slot is powered-off. In most cases the steps required to turn off the slot electrically (assert RST# to the slot, isolate the bus, power-off the slot) require only a short period of time (a few milliseconds) relative to the time required to insert the adapter card. Hardware protection schemes can be implemented that detect when the user begins an insertion operation and automatically turn off the slot to protect the hardware, if the user violates the proper insertion procedure.

6.4 Adapter Card Insertion and Removal Aids

The wide variety of legal sizes and shapes of PCI adapter cards, and tight card spacing can make it difficult to insert and remove a single card. Grasping a short adapter card located between two tall adapter cards can be particularly difficult. The process is even more difficult in a hot-plug system where the user must avoid contacting the tall cards at all, or risk causing an electrical short.

A good platform design must carefully consider the insertion and removal operation, and ways to simplify it. Some alternatives include:

•   Increased slot spacing. Increasing the spacing between the slots simplifies grasping the adapter card, and reduces the risk of disturbing neighboring cards.

•   Adapter card handles. Attaching grasping devices to the adapter card can make it easier to grasp the card for insertion and removal. Some handle designs can also act as spacers to reduce the risk of one card contacting another during the insertion or removal operation. The disadvantage of this approach is the difficulty of designing a handle that will attach to *any* standard adapter card outline. Furthermore, acquiring such handles and attaching them to every adapter card in the system would be a major inconvenience for the user.

7. Hot-Plug Platform Example

The Compaq ProLiant 6500, Compaq's first commercially available platform compliant with the Hot-Plug Spec, is a perfect example of the class of machine that can benefit from PCI hot-plug technology. The ProLiant 6500 supports four Pentium Pro processors, and up to 4 G bytes of main memory. The main chassis includes bays for up to seven disk drives, and eight PCI and EISA adapter cards, six of which are 32-bit, 33 MHz PCI hot-plug slots. This class of server can typically support hundreds of users in a networked environment, running mission-critical applications. Therefore, the ProLiant 6500 includes numerous features to increase the availability of the platform, and reduce the amount of downtime. To simplify reconfiguration of the server, and to survive certain kinds of failure and repair scenarios, the ProLiant 6500 includes hot-plug power supplies, hot-plug disk drivers, hot-plug ventilation fans, and, of course, PCI hot-plug slots.

This chapter describes the ProLiant 6500 as an example of how the alternatives available under the Hot-Plug Spec can be implemented.

7.1 Slot State and Attention Indicators

Figure 7-1 shows the externally visible feature of PCI hot-plug technology in the ProLiant 6500. Above each hot-plug slot are two LEDs. The green LED (farther from the PCI slot bracket) implements the slot state indicator, which is optional in the Hot-Plug Spec. Whenever the slot is on, the green LED will illuminate continuously. The amber LED (closer to the PCI slot bracket) implements the Attention Indicator, which is required by the Hot-Plug Spec. When the software determines that the card requires attention, the amber LED will illuminate continuously. Table 7-1 summarizes the four states of the two slot indicators.

By locating the slot indicators where they are visible from the rear of the unit, the ProLiant 6500 enables the user quickly to determine the states of all the hot-plug slots without opening the box. It also simplifies association of a particular slot requiring attention to any cable that might connect to the card. The slot indicators are also visible from inside the box to assist the user while inserting and removing adapter cards.

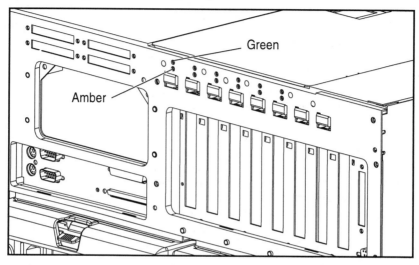

Figure 7-1: Slot State and Attention Indicators

LED States	Interpretation
GREEN ON AMBER OFF	The slot is on and functioning normally.
GREEN ON AMBER ON	The slot is on and the card requires attention.
GREEN OFF AMBER ON	The slot is off and the slot or the card in it requires attention.
GREEN OFF AMBER OFF	The slot is off and normal.

Table 7-1: Slot State and Attention Indicators

7.2 Physical Access and Protection

When the user must hot-remove or hot-insert an adapter card, he requires access to the hot-plug slot area, without exposure to other, hazardous areas of the server. Figure 7-2 illustrates the special access door in the Compaq ProLiant 6500 for accessing the hot-plug slots. Inside the door the user can access all of the hot-plug slots, but none of the other slots (EISA and conventional PCI slots). The walls of the area inside the door are insulated to prevent access to hazardous areas inside the chassis, and the system mother board is covered to prevent dropped items from contacting it.

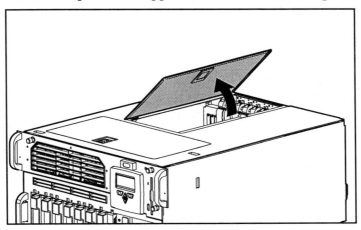

Figure 7-2: PCI Hot-Plug Slot Access Door

The slots in the ProLiant 6500 are spaced 1.0 inch apart, rather than the minimum 0.8-inch spacing that is possible in other designs. This increased slot spacing eases access to a short adapter card located between two tall ones, and provides room for the insulating dividers shown in Figure 7-3. Standing taller than a full-size PCI adapter card, and extending almost its full length, the dividers provide protection from accidental shorting between cards during the insertion and removal process. The dividers are attached only at the bottom, and are flexible enough that they deflect during insertion and removal to allow easy access to short adapter cards.

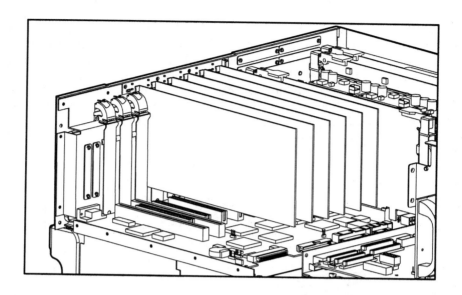

Figure 7-3: Slot Dividers

The ProLiant 6500 replaces the screws that commonly retain PCI cards with pivoting slot release levers shown in Figure 7-4. When a new adapter card is in place, the user rotates the lever down and latches it closed, clamping the adapter card in place. By depressing the latch at the top of the lever, the user can rotate the lever open to remove an adapter card.

A sensor attached to each hot-plug slot release lever informs the Hot-Plug Controller when the lever is open. The Hot-Plug Controller uses this information to guarantee that the slot is always powered-off before an adapter card is inserted.

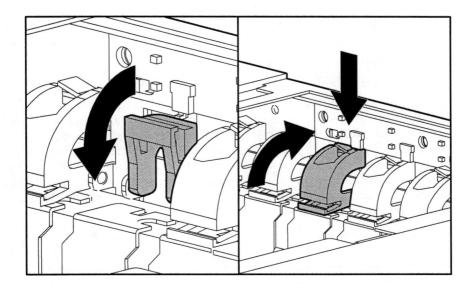

Figure 7-4: Slot Release Levers

7.3 Hot-Plug Controller

The ProLiant 6500 includes a PCI Hot-Plug Controller that is itself a PCI device. The PCI interface provides the Hot-Plug Controller the same advantages it provides to other devices, including low pin count, relocatable register addresses, and short bus transaction times. Although the ProLiant 6500 includes only one Hot-Plug Controller, implementing the Hot-Plug Controller as a PCI device helps solve a problem in systems with more than one Hot-Plug Controller. Coordinating which Hot-Plug Controller is associated with which hot-plug slots can be complicated in systems with more than one Hot-Plug Controller. The process is greatly simplified if the software can always assume that the Hot-Plug Controller is a PCI device on the same bus as the hot-plug slots it controls.

The ProLiant 6500 Hot-Plug Controller provides the following inputs and outputs for up to six hot-plug slots:

- Input for slot release lever
- Input for PRSNT[1:2]#
- Input for slot power fault detection circuitry

- Output for slot power enable
- Output for bus isolation device control
- Output for slot RST#
- Outputs for Slot State and Attention LEDs

The ProLiant 6500 Hot-Plug Controller provides high-level control for the hot-plug slots. Programmable registers determine whether the slots are fully on or fully off. Hardware sequencers inside the Hot-Plug Controller step through intermediate states and individually control the power, the bus-isolation, and the RST# pin for each slot. This kind of high-level control provided by the hardware insures that the software can never accidentally damage the hardware or leave a slot in an invalid state between off and on.

The ProLiant 6500 Hot-Plug Controller implements a single Base Address Register in its Configuration Space header, by which all of the Hot-Plug Controller's working registers are mapped into memory space. Table 7-2 shows the arrangement of the memory-mapped working registers.

Byte	31	bit		0
00h	Miscellaneous Control		Slot Enable	reserved
04h	reserved (write 0)	Amber LED Control	reserved (write 0)	Green LED Control
08h	Slot Input Interrupt and Clear			
	PRSNT[1]# bits	PRSNT[2]# bits	Power Faults	Slot Levers
0Ch	Slot Input Interrupt Mask			
	PRSNT[1]# mask bits	PRSNT[2]# mask bits	Power Fault mask bits	Slot Lever mask bits
10h	reserved			
14h	reserved			
18h	reserved			
1Ch	reserved			
20h	reserved			
24h	reserved			
28h	reserved	reserved	reserved	Slot mask

Table 7-2: Hot-Plug Controller Working Registers

The number of signals required to control six hot-plug slots is large enough that allocating a single pin in the Hot-Plug Controller package to each signal could become cost prohibitive. Therefore, many of the control registers in the ProLiant 6500 Hot-Plug Controller allow the control bits to be shifted serially into and out of the controller to minimize the number of pins required. In such implementations external shift registers latch and hold the serial control bits.

7.3.1 Slot Enable Register (memory offset 01h)

This working register provides the high-level control for turning the slots on and off. Each of the lower six bits in this register corresponds to the state of one of the hot-plug slots. Writing a new value to any of these bits, and then setting the Shift Output Go (SOGO) bit in the Miscellaneous Control register, will initiate a sequence of control steps that will turn a slot on or off according to the timing requirements of the Hot-Plug Spec.

The new value of this register is stored and compared to the old value each time the SOGO bit in the Miscellaneous Control register is set. If the value of one of these bits has changed from 0 to 1 when SOGO is set, the slot-on sequence is used to turn on that slot. If a value has changed from 1 to 0, the slot-off sequence is used to turn off that slot. If some bits have changed from 0 to 1 and others from 1 to 0 when SOGO is set, the appropriate slots are turned off first, and then the appropriate slots are turned on.

The current value of this register can be read back at any time, but may not indicate the current state of the slots if the SOGO bit has not yet been written, or if a previous slot-on or slot-off sequence has not yet completed.

All slots with closed slot release levers are enabled, when power is initially applied to the system. If a slot release lever opens for a slot that is turned on, the Hot-Plug Controller will automatically turn that slot off, and the Slot Enable bit for that slot will be held reset until the lever indicates the slot is closed.

Bit	Description
0	Enable slot A. 1 = enable.
1	Enable slot B. 1 = enable.
2	Enable slot C. 1 = enable.
3	Enable slot D. 1 = enable.
4	Enable slot E. 1 = enable.
5	Enable slot F. 1 = enable.
6	reserved
7	reserved

Table 7-3: Slot Enable Register

7.3.2 Miscellaneous Control Register (memory offset 02h)

Each bit in the Miscellaneous Control register performs a different function, as shown in Table 7-4.

Bit	Description
0	**Write: Shift Output Go (SOGO)** Writing a 1 to this bit (SOGO) while the Busy Status (SOBS) is a 0 will cause the slot control outputs to be updated from the latest contents of the LED and Slot Enable registers. Writing a 0 to this bit or writing a 1 while SOBS is a 1 is ignored. **Read: Shift Output Busy Status (SOBS)** When read (SOBS), this bit indicates the busy status of the shift output logic. SOBS is normally 0, but will be a 1 immediately after SOGO is written to a 1. SOBS will return to a 0 when the serial output operation is complete.
1	**Shift Output Interrupt Enable** When set to 1, the Hot-Plug Controller will generate an interrupt when SOBS changes from 1 to 0.
2	**Shift Output Interrupt Pending/Clear** When read as logic 1, this bit indicates that a Hot-Plug Controller interrupt was generated by SOBS changing from 1 to 0 while the Serial Output Interrupt Enable bit was set. Writing a 1 to this bit will clear this interrupt. Writing a 0 is ignored.
3	**Slot Input Interrupt Pending** After the Hot-Plug Controller generates an interrupt from one of the slot inputs, this bit will be a 1. When the interrupt is cleared, this bit will be a 0.
4-5	Reserved
6	**PCI Bus Frequency Range** 0 = 25MHz, 1 = 30/33MHz This bit is used to adjust internal time constants for things such as the 8 ms switch debounce timer.
7-15	Reserved

Table 7-4: Miscellaneous Control Register

7.3.3 LED Control Register (Green memory offset 04h, Amber memory offset 06h)

These registers provide control for the two LED devices for each hot-plug slot. A value of 1 corresponds to the on state of the LED. A value of 0 corresponds to the off state. After the desired state is programmed into the LED Control register, setting the Shift Output Go (SOGO) bit in the Miscellaneous Control register will cause the new LED state to take effect. Table 7-5 shows the locations of the bits in the LED Control register.

Bit	Function
0	Slot A LED
1	Slot B LED
2	Slot C LED
3	Slot D LED
4	Slot E LED
5	Slot F LED
6	reserved
7	reserved

Table 7-5: LED Control Registers

7.3.4 Slot Input Interrupt and Clear Register (memory offset 08h)

The software observes four input bits from each slot through this register. The bits can be programmed individually to be latched and cause an interrupt on any change of state, or the bits can be left unlatched and available to be read at any time without an interrupt.

When a slot input changes state (either high to low or low to high), and that bit is unmasked in the Slot Input Interrupt Mask Register, the Hot-Plug Controller generates an interrupt and the state of that slot input is latched in this register. A read of the register will find the current state of any non-interrupting (masked) bits, and the last-latched state of any interrupting (unmasked) bits. After the interrupt has been serviced, a write to this register with a logic one in the bit positions of each of the bits that were latched will clear the interrupt. Note that if another unmasked bit changes state between the time the software reads and writes this register, the new input will remain latched and the interrupt will remain pending.

Bit	Description
0	Slot release lever for slot A. 0 = lever closed (board installed)
1	Slot release lever for slot B. 0 = lever closed (board installed)
2	Slot release lever for slot C. 0 = lever closed (board installed)
3	Slot release lever for slot D. 0 = lever closed (board installed)
4	Slot release lever for slot E. 0 = lever closed (board installed)
5	Slot release lever for slot F. 0 = lever closed (board installed)
6	reserved (0)
7	reserved (0)
8	slot A power fault. 0 = fault
9	slot B power fault. 0 = fault
10	slot C power fault. 0 = fault
11	slot D power fault. 0 = fault
12	slot E power fault. 0 = fault
13	slot F power fault. 0 = fault
14	reserved (0)
15	reserved (0)
16	PRSNT[2]# for slot A
17	PRSNT[2]# for slot B
18	PRSNT[2]# for slot C
19	PRSNT[2]# for slot D
20	PRSNT[2]# for slot E
21	PRSNT[2]# for slot F
22	reserved (0)
23	reserved (0)
24	PRSNT[1]# for slot A
25	PRSNT[1]# for slot B
26	PRSNT[1]# for slot C
27	PRSNT[1]# for slot D
28	PRSNT[1]# for slot E
29	PRSNT[1]# for slot F
30	reserved (0)
31	reserved (0)

Table 7-6: Slot Input Interrupt and Clear Register

7.3.5 Slot Input Interrupt Mask Register (memory offset 0Ch)

The Slot Input Interrupt Mask register is used to control which inputs in the Slot Input Interrupt and Clear register should generate interrupts and which should not. If a state change occurs at a slot input while the mask bit for that input is set to a 1, no interrupt will be generated for that state change. If the mask bit is cleared, an interrupt will be generated on the next state change for that input. If an interrupt is currently being asserted for a bit that is unmasked, setting the mask bit will also clear the interrupt.

7.4 Slot Power Switches

The Compaq ProLiant 6500 uses one Harris Semiconductor HIP1011 for controlling the four power supply voltages for each hot-plug slot. The HIP1011 features integrated switches for +12V and -12V (+5V and +3.3V require external MOSFETs), over-current sensing on all supplies, under-voltage sensing on +5V, +3.3V, and +12V, and programmable turn-on voltage slew rate.

Figure 7-5 shows a typical application of the HIP1011. The power enable outputs from the Hot-Plug Controller connect to the PWRON inputs of the HP1011s for each slot. The +5V and the +3.3V supply voltages each require external MOSFETs, shown in the figure as two RF1K49211 transistors connected in parallel for each supply voltage. The value of the capacitor connected to the gates of these four MOSFETs determines the slew rate of the supply voltage, when power at the slot is turned on. Similar capacitors between the 12VO (+12V Output) and 12VG (+12V Gate), and M12VO (-12V Output) and M12VG (-12V Gate) determine the slew rates of the +12V and -12V supplies, respectively. The platform designer selects these capacitor values to set the supply voltage slew rates between the limits specified in the Hot-Plug Spec, as described in Section 3.6.2.

The HIP1011 senses the current drawn from the +5V and +3.3V supply voltages by measuring the voltage across the 10 mΩ resistor connected in series with each supply. Supply currents for the +12V and -12V supplies are sensed internally. All supply voltages except -12V are monitored for abnormally low voltages after the slot power is stable. If the HIP1011 senses either an over-current, or an under-voltage condition, it drives the FLTN pin low, and latches all of the output switches in the off state. The Compaq ProLiant 6500 connects the FLTN signals for each slot to the Slot Power Fault bits in the Slot Input Interrupt and Clear register of the Hot-Plug Controller, described in Section 7.3.

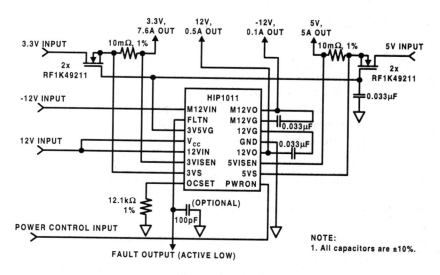

Figure 7-5: HIP1011 Typical Application[7]

7.5 Bus Isolation Devices

The Compaq ProLiant 6500 isolates most hot-plug slot signal pins
from the bus with Texas Instruments SN74CBT6800, 10-Bit
Crossbar Switches with Precharged Outputs for Live Insertion.
Figure 7-6 shows a simplified logic diagram of the part. The bus-
connection control pins from the Hot-Plug Controller are connected
to the ON- pins of each SN74CBT6800. The A side of the component
connects to the PCI bus, and the B side to the hot-plug slot. BIASV
is the bias voltage pin, and connects to the +5V supply voltage for
the slot.

When the Hot-Plug Controller drives the ON- pin low, the FETs
between the A and B sides of the SN74CBT6800 turn on, providing
a low impedance connection (approximately 5 Ω) between the slot
and the bus. When the ON- pin is high, the FETs between the A
and B sides turn off, isolating the slot from the bus, and the FETs
between the B side and the BIASV pin turn on. In the conducting
state the bias FETs behave approximately like 10 KΩ resistors.
Since the ProLiant 6500 connects the BIASV pin to the +5V supply

---

[7] Copyrighted by Harris Corporation, reprinted with permission of Harris
Corporation Semiconductor Sector.

voltage for the slot, the biased connector signal pins will be pulled to the +5V supply rail as it rises or falls.

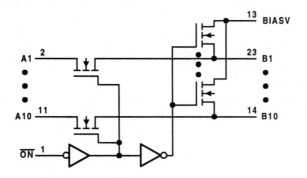

Figure 7-6: SN74CBT6800 10-Bit Crossbar Switch[8]

---

[8] Courtesy of Texas Instruments.

8. Hot-Plug Software Examples

This chapter presents example implementations of the Hot-Plug Spec in three different operating systems. The architecture of each of these operating systems is quite different, leading to differences in the implementations of hot-plug technology. The architecture of each system is presented, and whenever possible, specific software module and operation names are associated with the generic names presented in the Hot-Plug Spec.

Any discussion of a current, commercial operating system will quickly become out of date as new releases expand or modify older functionality. This chapter is not intended to provide information at the detail required to write hot-plug-ready adapter drivers. Only documentation from the operating system vendor could do that. This chapter illustrates how the principles and requirements of the Hot-Plug Spec were first implemented in real applications. It is expected that hot-plug support under each of these operating systems will continue to expand and improve.

8.1 Novell IntranetWare

Figure 8-1 shows some of the internal architecture of IntranetWare. The unshaded areas in the figure show the standard portions of IntranetWare that exist in conventional, non-hot-plug systems. The shaded areas are the new modules added according to the Hot-Plug Spec. As can be seen from the figure, the natural modularity of Novell IntranetWare enabled PCI hot-plug capabilities to be integrated easily. Most changes involved adding new modules rather than modifying existing ones. Few kernel changes were required, and only minor enhancements were required in the conventional drivers and their interface architectures, ODI and NWPA.

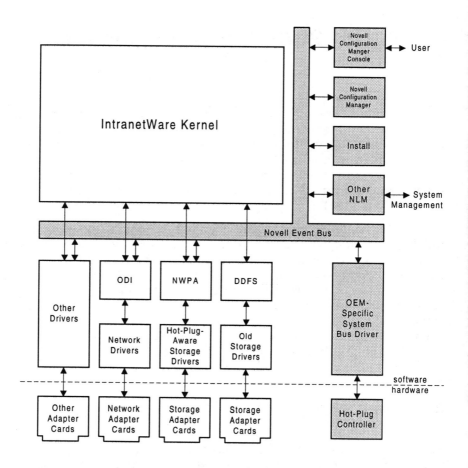

Figure 8-1: Novell IntranetWare Hot-Plug Architecture

Table 8-1 lists all the components in Figure 8-1, along with a brief definition, and the corresponding component from the Hot-Plug Spec, as shown in Figure 2-1 in Chapter 2.

Component of Hot-Plug IntranetWare (Figure 8-1)	Definition	Corresponding Component of the Hot-Plug Spec (Figure 2-1)
IntranetWare Kernel	All of the operating system not otherwise detailed in the figure.	Operating System
Other Drivers	Device drivers other than those for network or storage devices.	Adapter Driver
ODI	Open Data-link Interface. Interface module for network device drivers.	
Network Driver	Communication network device driver.	Adapter Driver
Network Adapter Card	Communication network interface hardware.	Adapter Card
NWPA	NetWare Peripheral Architecture. Interface module for storage device drivers.	
Hot-plug-aware Storage Drivers	Storage device driver that has been modified to support hot-removal and hot-insertion.	Adapter Driver
Storage Adapter Card	Interface hardware for a storage device	Adapter Card
DDFS	Device Driver Functional Specification. Predecessor to NWPA.	
Old Storage Driver	Device driver for storage device written prior to NWPA.	Adapter Driver
OEM-Specific System Bus Driver	Device driver for the Hot-Plug Controller.	Hot-Plug System Driver
Hot-Plug Controller	Hardware that controls hot-plug operations on the platform.	Hot-Plug Controller
Novell Event Bus	A communication channel for signaling between modules. Carries hot-plug primitives as well as other messages.	Hot-Plug Primitives, Management Agent API
Novell Configuration Manager Console	User interface for hot-plug operations.	Hot-Plug Service
Novell Configuration Manager	Manages hot-plug operations. Controls quiesce sequence, and starting new device drivers.	Hot-Plug Service
Installation Tool	Locates the appropriate device driver for a newly installed device.	Hot-Plug Service
Other NetWare Loadable Modules	Other applications that can be loaded under IntranetWare.	

Table 8-1: Components of Hot-Plug IntranetWare

8.1.1 Key IntranetWare Components

ODI

The Open Data-Link Interface (ODI) is an interface module between the IntranetWare kernel and all network device drivers. Its specification defines the driver architecture for network devices. In previous versions of IntranetWare the ODI specification did not allow a single network driver instance to be unloaded without unloading *all* instances of the same driver. In other words, there was no way to stop using a single network adapter without stopping the use of all other network adapters controlled by the same driver.

Version 3.31 of the ODI specification adds a new interface to the Novell Event Bus for sending and receiving messages for hot-plug operations (such as quiescing the adapter driver). It also specifies driver modifications to allow a single driver instance to be unloaded while the rest remain operational.

Network Driver

A network device driver controls communication-network adapter hardware used in local-area and wide-area networks. Minimal changes are required in IntranetWare device drivers to allow a single instance of a device driver to be shut down for a hot-removal operation.

NWPA

The NetWare Peripheral Architecture (NWPA) is an interface module between the IntranetWare kernel and storage device drivers. Its specification defines the driver architecture for storage devices. In previous versions of IntranetWare neither NWPA nor its predecessor, Device Driver Functional Specification (DDFS), allowed a single storage driver instance to be unloaded without unloading *all* instances of the same driver. In other words, there was no way to stop using a single storage adapter without stopping the use of all other storage adapters controlled by the same driver.

Version 2.32 of the NWPA specification adds a new interface to the Novell Event Bus for sending and receiving messages for hot-plug operations (such as quiescing the adapter driver). It also specifies driver modifications to allow a single driver instance to be unloaded while the rest remain operational.

Hot-Plug-Aware Storage Drivers

Hot-plug-aware storage device drivers communicate with the NWPA module and control storage device hardware. They differ from previous versions of IntranetWare storage drivers in that they support single-instance unload. These device drivers will still load and operate normally on a conventional platform.

DDFS

The Device Driver Functional Specification (DDFS) is the predecessor to NWPA. Conventional storage device drivers written to the DDFS specification can still be loaded and operated normally in a hot-plug system, but do not enable hot-plugging of their devices.

Old Storage Driver

A storage device driver written for the DDFS specification. Storage device drivers written to the DDFS specification can still be loaded and operated normally in a hot-plug system.

OEM-Specific System Bus Driver

The OEM-Specific System Bus Driver (SBD) is the device driver for the Hot-Plug Controller. The generic term for this driver in the Hot-Plug Spec is Hot-Plug System Driver. The IntranetWare architecture allows multiple SBDs to exist simultaneously. Each platform vendor will supply an SBD for his hot-plug platform.

IntranetWare relies upon the system's boot ROM (provided by the platform vendor) to initialize the PCI Configuration Space headers for all PCI devices when power is initially applied to the system. Similarly, after a hot-insertion event IntranetWare relies on the other piece of platform-vendor software, the SBD, to initialize the adapter card's Configuration Space headers. The initial implementation of hot-plug functionality in IntranetWare supported only replacing one adapter card with another of the same type. With this version the contents of the Configuration Space header is saved when the old card is hot-removed, and restored when the new one is hot-inserted. Newer versions of the IntranetWare hot-plug support modules implement hot-addition. In these versions the SBD is responsible for assigning new memory and I/O ranges for a newly added adapter card.

Novell Event Bus

A central component in the hot-plug IntranetWare architecture is the Novell Event Bus (NEB). It is a software bus for communicating messages between the administrator, the software modules, management agents, and device drivers. The first implementation of the event bus is a NetWare Loadable Module (NLM), so it can be added easily to existing versions of IntranetWare. Future versions of IntranetWare will integrate the NEB into the kernel.

Novell Configuration Manager Console

The Novell Configuration Manager (NCM) Console provides the user interface for hot-plug operations. The console provides information to the user about the status of each slot and adapter card, and the user enters commands at this console to turn slots on and off.

The NCM Console consists of two screens, the Main Menu and Slot Detail Information. The Main Menu displays a list of all PCI slots (both hot-plug and conventional) in the system, and displays the following information:

- Slot number
- Whether the slot is a hot-plug or a conventional slot
- Product name or description of the adapter card
- Operational status of the slot or adapter card

Selecting a particular slot and pressing the Enter key on the keyboard will display a list of slot options (Remove, Replace, Add, or displaying the Slot Detail Information), as shown in Figure 8-2.

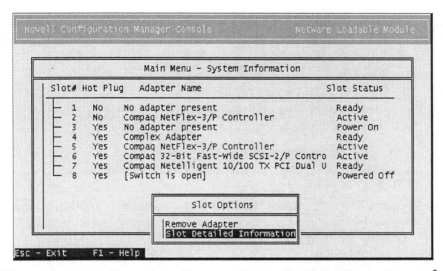

Figure 8-2: Configuration Manager Console Main Menu Screen[9]

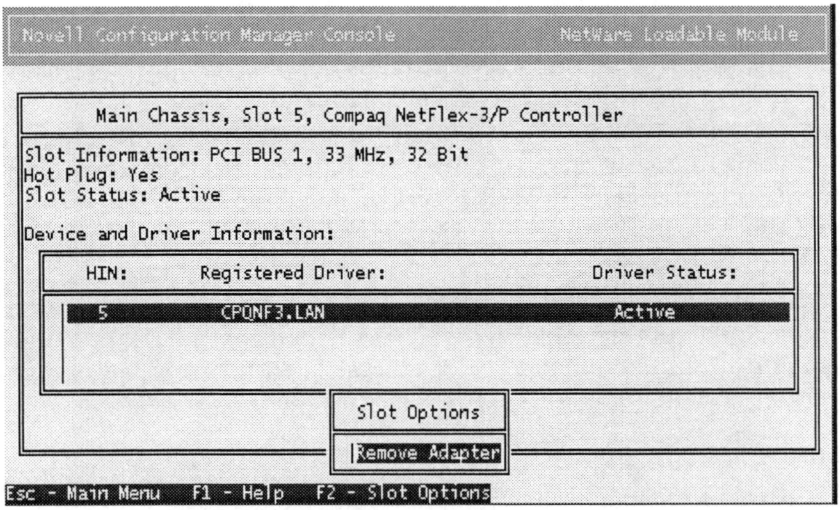

Figure 8-3: Configuration Manager Console Slot Detail Screen[10]

---

[9] Compaq, "PCI Hot Plug Technology with Novell Architecture," March 21, 1997, Document number 131A/0397.

[10] Compaq, "PCI Hot Plug Technology with Novell Architecture," March 21, 1997, Document number 131A/0397.

The Slot Detail Information screen displays additional information about a specific slot and the adapter card in that slot. This information includes the following:

- Slot number
- Adapter card name and description
- Bus number and bus type associated with that slot
- Whether the slot is a hot-plug or a conventional slot
- Operational status of the slot or adapter
- Device and driver information associated with the adapter card

Pressing the F2 key on the keyboard activates the Slot Option menu, as shown in Figure 8-3, which allows the user to take actions such as removing or replacing the adapter card in that slot.

Novell Configuration Manager

The Novell Configuration Manager (NCM) plays a central role in hot-plug operations. When an adapter card is hot-removed, the NCM is responsible for identifying and properly shutting down the adapter card's device driver (or drivers, if the card contains multiple devices) before turning off the slot. The NCM sends messages over the Novell Event Bus to the drivers (by way of the NWPA or ODI support modules), notifying them to quiesce adapter activity. After adapter activity is quiesced the NCM sends Hot-Plug Primitive messages over the Novell Event Bus to the OEM-Specific System Bus Driver (SBD) to turn off the slot.

When an adapter card is hot-inserted, the NCM sends messages to the SBD to turn the slot on and initialize the adapter card's Configuration Space header or headers. Then it sends a message to the Installation Tools to automatically find and load a driver.

Installation Tool

The Installation Tool is used to locate the required device driver for an adapter card. In initial implementations this was a manual process. Current implementations automatically determine the need for additional device drivers, when adding adapter cards to the system.

Other NetWare Loadable Modules

Other NetWare Loadable Modules (NLMs) can register to send and receive messages over the Novell Event Bus (NEB). Figure 8-1 illustrates one application of this feature as an interface to a remote system management console, from which an administrator could perform the same operations as the user at the Novell Configuration Manager Console.

8.1.2 Use of the Novell Event Bus

The Novell Event Bus (NEB) carries a wide variety of event messages between the various hot-plug software modules. Any NetWare Loadable Module (NLM) can produce and consume messages on the NEB. Production and consumption of messages is independent. The producing module can be blind to the identity of the consuming module. Each software module involved with hot-plug operations will register with the NEB while loading, identifying which messages it can receive. When a module sends a message to the NEB, the NEB forwards it to all modules registered to receive that kind of message. For example, the OEM-Specific System Bus Driver (SBD) is responsible for turning off a slot after adapter activity has been quiesced. When the SBD loads, it registers with the NEB to receive all messages to turn off a slot. When the Novell Configuration Manager is ready to turn off a slot, it sends the appropriate message to the NEB. The NEB then forwards the message to the SBD.

To illustrate the messages on the NEB, Table 8-2 shows a subset of the NEB messages that are handled by the SBD. The SBD is what the Hot-Plug Spec calls the Hot-Plug System Driver, and the messages it handles are called Hot-Plug Primitives. Table 8-2 shows each message related to a Hot-Plug Primitive.

NEB Message	Description	Hot-Plug Primitive
HW.SlotShutdown	Request to turn off the specified slot. The SBD should consume this message if it controls the specified slot. Upon completion, the SBD must send an HW.SlotShutdownReply.	Setting Slot Status
HW.SlotShutdownReply	Reply to a previous request to shutdown a slot (HW.SlotShutdown). This is produced by the SBD after the slot it off.	Setting Slot Status
HW.SlotStatusChange	Notification that the status of the slot has changed. The SBD should produce this message whenever there is a change in slot status that was not a result of a HW.SlotShutdown or HW.SlotInitialize.	Asynchronous Notification of Slot Status Change
HW.SlotInitialize	Request to turn on a slot and initialize the adapter card Configuration Space header for the device(s) found there. An SBD should consume this message if it controls the specified slot. When the slot is turned on and the device(s) configured, the SBD must send an HW.SlotInitializeReply.	Setting Slot Status
HW.SlotInitializeReply	Reply to a previous request to initialize a slot (HW.SlotInitialize). If the slot was powered-on successfully, the approximately 1-second delay from RST# to first access (discussed in Section 3.5.1) has elapsed, and the adapter card's Configuration Space is initialized.	Setting Slot Status
HW.PCI.RequestSlotStatus	Request for detailed information on a slot. An SBD must consume this message if it controls the indicated slot, and respond with HW.PCI.ReplySlotStatus.	Getting Slot Status
HW.PCI.ReplySlotStatus	Reply to HW.PCI.RequestSlotStatus with detailed slot information.	Getting Slot Status

Table 8-2: Hot-Plug Primitives on the Novell Event Bus

8.2 Microsoft Windows NT

Compaq's implementation of hot-plug software under Windows NT 4.0 illustrates another way that hot-plug support can be delivered to the user. Although Compaq generally produces platforms, not operating systems, Compaq developed hot-plug support for Window NT 4.0 by adding new modules and modifying device drivers, without modifying the kernel. This approach minimized development cost, and simplified acceptance of the new technology by those already using Windows NT 4.0. Support for hot-plug operations under Windows NT 5.0 is discussed briefly at the end of this section.

Windows NT treats resource allocation and PCI device configuration as operating system functions. Allocating resources for a new device outside of the operating system would be quite complicated. Therefore, this implementation of hot-plug technology in Windows NT 4.0 supports only replacing one adapter card for another one of the same type, one that uses the same Configuration Space resources and device driver. This enables the software to remember the contents of the Configuration Space header before an adapter card is hot-removed, and to restore those contents when the replacement card is hot-inserted. It is expected that future versions of NT will integrate hot-plug support more tightly with the operating system, and will support the hot-addition of new adapter card.

Figure 8-4 illustrates the major components of Windows NT 4.0 related to hot-plug operations, as implemented by Compaq. The shaded components are the new hot-plug components. Table 8-3 lists all the software components from Figure 8-4, along with a brief definition and, where appropriate, the corresponding component from the Hot-Plug Spec, as shown in Figure 2-1 in Chapter 2.

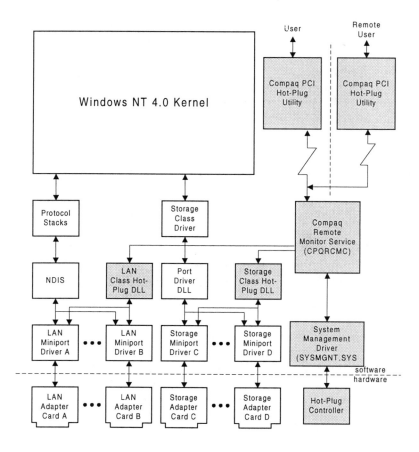

Figure 8-4: Compaq Hot-Plug Architecture for Microsoft Windows NT 4.0

Component of Hot-Plug Windows NT 4.0 (Figure 8-4)	Definition	Corresponding Component of the Hot-Plug Spec (Figure 2-1)
Windows NT 4.0 Kernel	All of the operating system not otherwise detailed in the figure.	Operating System
Protocol Stacks	Software layer responsible for managing the network protocols.	
NDIS	Network Driver Interface Specification. Software layer responsible for managing network protocols.	
LAN Miniport Driver	Local Area Network device driver. Modified to accept hot-plug requests from the LAN Class Hot-Plug DLL.	Adapter Driver
LAN Adapter Card	Local Area Network interface hardware.	Adapter Card
LAN Class Hot-Plug DLL	Software layer (dynamic link library) that provides a standard interface between the Compaq Remote Monitor Service and all LAN miniport drivers.	
Storage Class Driver	Software layer responsible for managing storage device protocols	
Port Driver DLL	Software layer that provides a standard interface between the Storage Class Driver and all the storage miniport drivers.	
Storage Miniport Driver	Storage device driver. Modified to accept hot-plug requests from the Storage Class Hot-Plug DLL.	Adapter Driver
Storage Class Hot-Plug DLL	Software layer (dynamic link library) that provides a standard interface between the Compaq Remote Monitor Service and all storage miniport drivers.	
Compaq PCI Hot-Plug Utility	Provides the user interface to hot-plug functions. Can be run from remote locations.	Hot-Plug Service
Compaq Remote Monitor Service	Manages hot-plug operations. Controls quiesce sequence, and starting new device drivers.	Hot-Plug Service
System Management Driver	Device driver for the Hot-Plug Controller.	Hot-Plug System Driver
Hot-Plug Controller	Hardware that controls hot-plug operations on the platform.	Hot-Plug Controller

Table 8-3: Components of Hot-Plug Windows NT 4.0

8.2.1 Key Windows NT 4.0 Components

Protocol Stacks

This software layer is responsible for managing the network protocols. No modifications are required to this module to support hot-plug capabilities.

NDIS

The Network Driver Interface Specification (NDIS) defines a software layer that provides a standard interface between the protocol stacks and LAN miniport drivers. No modifications are required to this module to support hot-plug capabilities.

LAN Miniport Driver

A local-area network miniport device driver controls network adapter hardware. Standard network device drivers must be modified to accept quiesce and resume requests from the Compaq Remote Monitor Service. Once such a driver is quiesced it will not accept any more requests from the NDIS layer to use the adapter card.

LAN Class Hot-Plug DLL

This module is the DLL (dynamic link library) that provides a standard interface between the Compaq Remote Monitor Service and all LAN miniport drivers.

Storage Class Driver

This software layer manages the protocol for storage class devices. No modifications are required to this module to support hot-plug capabilities.

Port Driver DLL

This module is a DLL (dynamic link library) that provides a standard interface between the Storage Class Driver and all the storage miniport drivers. No modifications are required to this module to support hot-plug capabilities.

Storage Miniport Driver

A storage miniport device driver controls storage adapter hardware. Standard storage device drivers must be modified to accept quiesce and resume requests from the Compaq Remote Monitor Service. Once such a driver is quiesced it will not accept any more requests from the Port Driver layer to use the adapter card.

Storage Class Hot-Plug DLL

This module is the DLL (dynamic link library) that provides a standard interface between the Compaq Remote Monitor Service and all storage miniport drivers.

Compaq PCI Hot-Plug Utility

The Compaq PCI Hot-Plug Utility, or simply the Utility, provides the primary means for the user to access the hot-plug functionality of the system. The Utility can be run either on the platform that contains the hot-plug slots or from a remote location over a network connection.

Figure 8-5 shows the primary screen that provide information to the user about the slots, and permits the user to change certain aspects of the slots (like turning slots on and off). This screen displays the following information for each hot-plug slot:

- Whether the slot is presently on or off. The symbol to the far left of the slot number corresponds to the slot-state LED of that slot. The LED symbol is green when the slot it on, and gray when the slot is off.

- Whether the Attention Indicator for the slot is on or off. The symbol to the immediate right of the slot number corresponds to the slot Attention Indicator. The LED symbol is amber when the slot's Attention Indicator is on, and gray when the slot's Attention Indicator is off.

- Slot number

- Product name or description of the adapter card

- Operational status of the slot or adapter card

Microsoft Windows NT

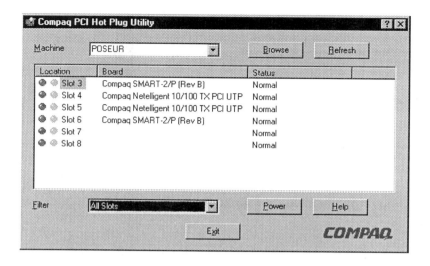

Figure 8-5: Compaq PCI Hot-Plug Utility User Interface for Windows NT 4.0[11]

This screen provides additional capability as described in Table 8-4.

Function	Description
Browse	Selects the system being viewed and managed by the utility (as described in a later section).
Refresh	Manually triggers a screen update.
Power	Switches off and on the power for the individual hot plug slots.
Help	Invokes the PCI Hot Plug specific help page.
Filter	Used to select the criteria determining which PCI Hot Plug slots are shown by the utility.

Table 8-4: PCI Hot-Plug Utility Primary Functions[12]

Compaq Remote Monitor Service

The Compaq Remote Monitor Service, or simply the Service, plays a central roll in hot-plug operations. When an adapter card is hot-

[11] Compaq, "Deploying PCI Hot Plug on Compaq Servers in a Microsoft Windows NT Environment," July 1997, Document number 064A/0797.
[12] Compaq, "Deploying PCI Hot Plug on Compaq Servers in a Microsoft Windows NT Environment," July 1997, Document number 064A/0797.

removed, the Service is responsible for identifying and properly shutting down the device driver before turning off the slot. The Service sends requests via the appropriate class hot-plug DLL to notify the driver to quiesce adapter activity. After adapter activity is quiesced the service sends requests to the System Management Driver to turn off the slot. When an adapter card is hot-inserted, the Service sends requests to the System Management Driver to turn the slot on and initialize the card.

The interface between the Service and the System Management Driver (the Hot-Plug Primitives) is implemented at a very low level. Most of the intelligence for controlling the Hot-Plug Controller resides in the Service. The Service generally turns slots on and off by issuing set and reset requests addressing specific bits in specific registers within the Hot-Plug Controller. This approach has the unusual side effect of customizing the Service to a particular Hot-Plug Controller. This kind of register-level bit manipulation is commonly managed by the device driver, so the application can be kept generic and portable. However portability was unnecessary in this case, since the entire hot-plug software solution was developed by the platform vendor (rather than the operating system vendor), thereby limiting its application to a single platform-vendor's hardware.

The Service is also responsible for saving and restoring the Configuration Space header for each adapter driver that supports hot-plug operations. When the Service first loads and identifies a hot-plug-ready adapter driver, the Service uses the System Management Driver to retrieve the current Configuration Space header information for each device on that adapter card. After an adapter card is removed and reinserted, the Service verifies that the replacement card is of the same type as the one removed, and passes the stored Configuration Space header information back to the System Management Driver to be rewritten to the adapter card.

System Management Driver

The System Management Driver is the device driver for the Hot-Plug Controller. The generic term for this driver in the Hot-Plug Spec is Hot-Plug System Driver.

8.2.2 Microsoft Windows NT 5.0

The next release of Windows NT is planned to include PCI hot-plug support built into the operating system. PCI hot-plug technology compliments several other technologies also planned to be included in the same release. Expanded plug-and-play capability will simplify assigning resources to a new device, enabling hot-add capability. Furthermore, the development of the Advance Configuration and Power Interface (ACPI) standard for operating-system-directed power management standardizes many of the mechanisms for powering-off a subset of the system, and restoring power and reconfiguring it. PCI hot-plug operations are very similar to power-management operations, and should use many of the same control mechanisms.

Similarities between power-management and hot-plug operations also lead to similar new requirements for adapter drivers. It is expected that device drivers written to support the standard Windows NT 5.0 Driver Development Kit (DDK) functionality will be ready for hot-plug operations as well as power management operations.

8.3 SCO UnixWare 7

The most recent major release of the UNIX operating system from SCO is UnixWare 7. UnixWare 7 is the first step in the evolution of SCO OpenServer 5 and UnixWare 2.

UnixWare 7 includes many features useful to high-performance file and application servers. It supports symmetric multiprocessing (SMP) systems, large memory and file systems, and clustering. To improve system reliability and data integrity UnixWare 7 supports journaling file systems, disk spanning and mirroring, multiple redundant paths to storage subsystems, hot-swap disk drives, monitoring of uninterruptable power supplies, and of course, PCI hot-plug technology.

Figure 8-6 shows some of the internal architecture of UnixWare 7. The unshaded areas in the figure show the standard portions of UnixWare 7 that apply to conventional as well as hot-plug systems. The shaded areas are the new modules added according to the Hot-Plug Spec. The resource allocation and device configuration portions of the UnixWare 7 kernel include significant enhancements to enable devices to be installed and removed while the system is running. Enhancements were also required in the conventional drivers and their interface modules, LAN (or MAC) Driver Interface (MDI) and Storage Driver Interface (SDI), to make them ready for PCI hot-plug applications.

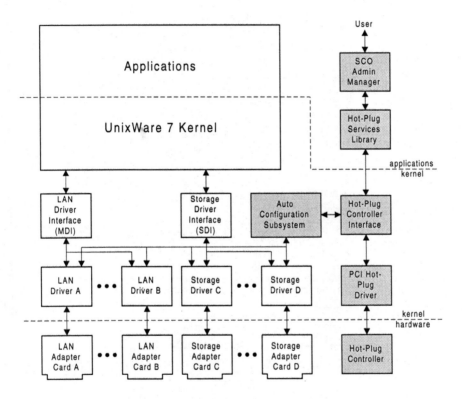

Figure 8-6: SCO UnixWare 7 PCI Hot-Plug Architecture

Table 8-5 lists the major components in Figure 8-6, along with a brief definition, and the corresponding component from the Hot-Plug Spec, as shown in Figure 2-1 in Chapter 2.

Component of Hot-Plug SCO UnixWare 7 (Figure 8-6)	Definition	Corresponding Component of the Hot-Plug Spec (Figure 2-1)
UnixWare 7 Kernel	All of the operating system not otherwise detailed in the figure.	Operating System
LAN Driver Interface (MDI)	Interface module for LAN device drivers. MDI is MAC (Media Access Controller) Driver Interface.	
LAN Driver	Local Area Network device driver.	Adapter Driver
LAN Adapter Card	Local Area Network interface hardware.	Adapter Card
Storage Driver Interface (SDI)	Interface module for storage device drivers.	
Storage Driver	Storage device driver.	Adapter Driver
Storage Adapter Card	Interface hardware for a storage device	Adapter Card
PCI Hot-Plug Driver	Device driver for the Hot-Plug Controller.	Hot-Plug System Driver
Hot-Plug Controller	Hardware that controls hot-plug operations on the platform.	Hot-Plug Controller
SCO Admin Manager	User interface for hot-plug operations.	Hot-Plug Service
Config Driver	Provides kernel-mode access to resources and routines for performing hot-plug operations such as quiescing and resuming drivers and turning slots off and on.	Hot-Plug Service
Hot-Plug Services Library	Provides a standard user-mode interface between the SCO Admin Manager and the rest of the system to provide access to resources and routines for performing hot-plug operations such as quiescing and resuming drivers and turning slots off and on.	Hot-Plug Service
Auto Configuration Subsystem	Manages device type and resource allocation. Sends messages to device drivers to bind them to specific devices.	Hot-Plug Service

Table 8-5: Components of Hot-Plug Support in SCO UnixWare 7

8.3.1 Key Hot-Plug UnixWare 7 Components

LAN Driver Interface (MDI)

The LAN, or MAC (Media Access Controller) Driver Interface (MDI) is an interface module between the UnixWare 7 kernel and all network device drivers.

LAN Driver and Storage Driver

A local-area network device driver communicates with the MDI module and controls network adapter hardware. Storage device drivers communicate with the SDI module and control storage device hardware.

In SCO UnixWare 7, the device driver architecture (including LAN and storage drivers) is defined by the Device Driver Interface (DDI) specification. UnixWare 7 is both binary- and source-compatible with device drivers written according to previous versions of the DDI specification, version DDI-5 through DDI-8.

New hot-plug functionality is defined in DDI-8. Device drivers must be written according to DDI-8 to support hot-plug operations. Previous versions of the DDI specification did not support suspending a device driver. Furthermore, when a device driver was loaded, there was no way to bind the driver to a single instance of a particular adapter card without affecting all other identical adapter cards. DDI-8 allows a driver instance that corresponds to a single adapter card to be added or removed at any time. DDI-8 also allows a driver instance to be suspended while an adapter card is removed, and then the same driver instance to be resumed once the replacement card is inserted.

SDI

The Storage Device Interface (SDI) is an interface module between the UnixWare 7 kernel and storage device drivers.

PCI Hot-Plug Driver

The PCI Hot-Plug Driver (PHPD) is the device driver for the Hot-Plug Controller. The generic term for this driver in the Hot-Plug Spec is Hot-Plug System Driver. The UnixWare 7 architecture allows multiple PHPDs to exist simultaneously. Each platform vendor will supply a PHPD for his hot-plug platform.

UnixWare 7 relies upon the system BIOS (provided by the platform vendor) to initialize the PCI Configuration Space headers for all PCI devices when power is initially applied to the system. Similarly, after a hot-insertion event (either a new addition or a replacement of a previously removed card) UnixWare 7 relies on the other piece of platform-vendor software, the PHPD, to initialize the adapter card's Configuration Space headers. All Configuration Space header information must be initialized before the PHPD completes a slot-on command. Although the Hot-Plug Spec permits the operating system to accept partial adapter card configuration, UnixWare 7 does not allow it. If an adapter card's Configuration Space header information cannot be completely initialized, the PHPD will turn the slot off and notify the UnixWare 7 kernel that it was unable to configure the card because of insufficient PCI resources.

SCO Admin Manager

The SCO Admin Manager provides the user interface and most sequencing and control for hot-plug operations. The Admin Manager can operate either with a graphical or a character-based interface. It provides information to the user about the status of each slot and adapter card, and enables the user to quiesce and resume drivers and to turn slots on and off.

The SCO Admin Manager has a single main screen, shown in Figure 8-7 that lists all the PCI hot-plug slots and any drivers currently in the suspended state. (Drivers are generally suspended while the user replaces one adapter card with another that will use the same driver.) The main screen shows the following information for each hot-plug slot:

- Slot state (on or off).

- Attention indicator state (normal or attention).

- The state of the slot interlock mechanism (if the platform provides one)

- Whether an adapter card is present in the slot.

- Slot number.

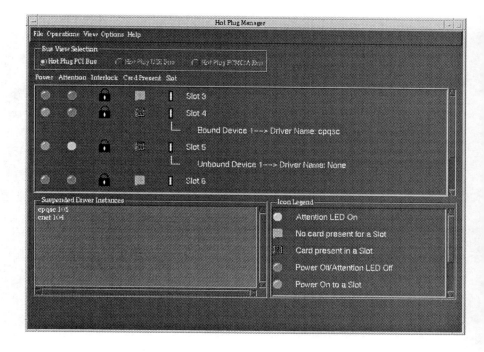

Figure 8-7: SCO Admin Manager Main Screen

When an adapter card is present in a slot and the slot is turned on, each PCI function on that adapter card will have an additional line containing the following information:

- A device descriptions based on the PCI class code, e.g. "empty slot," "SCSI bus controller," "RAID controller," "Ethernet controller," etc.

- An indication of whether a driver is bound to the device.

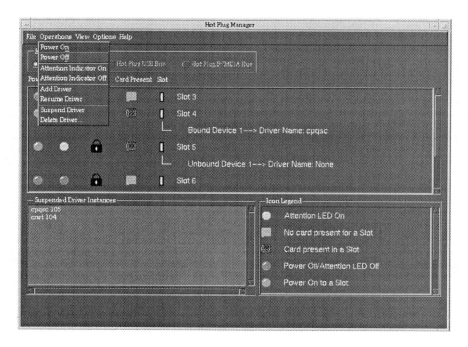

Figure 8-8: Hot-Plug Operations Menu

Most hot-plug operations appear in the pull-down menu under the "Operations" button on the main screen, as shown in Figure 8-8. Operations on the slot hardware are separated from operations on devices or device drivers. On the slot hardware the user can perform the following operations:

- Turn a slot on.
- Turn a slot off (if the driver has previously been quiesced or suspended).
- Turn an attention indicator on.
- Turn an attention indicator off.

On a device and device driver the user can perform the following operations:

- Add a driver instance; *i.e.*, cause the driver instance to begin using the device.
- Resume using a driver instance that was previously suspended while an adapter card was replaced.

- Suspend a driver instance; *i.e.*, quiesce device activity without removing that service from the system.

- Remove a driver instance; *i.e.*, remove the service that this device is providing to the system. The system will first perform a suspend operation on this driver instance (if it is not already suspended) to avoid data loss.

Hot-Plug Services Library and Hot-Plug Controller Interface

The Hot-Plug Services Library and the Hot-Plug Controller Interface provide a standard interface between the Admin Manager and the rest of the system. The Services Library links with the SCO Admin Manager, and provides access not only to the Controller Interface, but also to other system resources for operations such as discovering what drivers are available to be loaded for a particular device.

Controller Interface executes in kernel-mode, and provides access to privileged resources such as the PCI Hot-Plug Driver, and adapter drivers (through the Autoconfiguration Subsystem). The Hot-Plug Primitives that control the slot hardware come through the Controller Interface to the Services Library. Messages to the adapter drivers to quiesce suspend, or resume come through the Controller Interface to the Autoconfiguration Subsystem.

Autoconfiguration Subsystem

The Autoconfiguration Subsystem is a collection of routines that identify devices and determine which device drivers are appropriate to bind to them. It is designed to discover devices at system boot time and produces a resource database, which contains information about the configuration of adapter cards in the system. This resource database is used to determine which device drivers are loaded and run.

The Autoconfiguration Subsystem was enhanced in UnixWare 7 to support the dynamic addition and removal of devices (through hot plug operations) and updating the resource database accordingly.

9. Index

Notes

Notes

Notes

Notes

Related books from Annabooks

PCI Hardware and Software, Fourth Edition
Exceeds PCI Local Bus Specification 2.2

USB Peripheral Design
Developing USB PC Peripherals

Coming Soon

PCI Power Management Hardware and Software
USB Hardware and Software

Annabooks

11838 Bernardo Plaza Court

San Diego, CA 92128

619-673-0870   800-462-1042   619-673-1432 FAX

http://www.annabooks.com

Please send comments to feedback@annabooks.com